HAPPY RELATIONSHIPS

25 Buddhist Practices to Transform Your Connection with Your Partner, Family, and Friends

KIMBERLY BROWN

Prometheus Books

Essex, Connecticut

 Prometheus Books

An imprint of The Globe Pequot Publishing Group, Inc.
64 South Main St.
Essex, CT 06426
www.prometheusbooks.com

Distributed by NATIONAL BOOK NETWORK

British Library Cataloguing in Publication Information Available

Library of Congress Cataloging-in-Publication Data

Names: Brown, Kimberly, 1964– author.
Title: Happy relationships: 25 Buddhist practices to transform your connections with your partner, family, and friends / Kimberly Brown.
Description: Essex, Connecticut: Prometheus, [2025] | Summary: "A relatable and useful guide with practical applications to help readers stay attuned with their dearest people. Using simple tools drawn from the Buddhist tradition, readers can cultivate appreciation, set wise expectations, and create meaningful and intimate bonds of mutual support and kindness with their partners, families, and friends"—Provided by publisher.
Identifiers: LCCN 2024032772 (print) | LCCN 2024032773 (ebook) | ISBN 9781493086603 (paper) | ISBN 9781493086610 (epub)
Subjects: LCSH: Interpersonal relations. | Social interaction. | Buddhism.
Classification: LCC HM1106 .B767 2025 (print) | LCC HM1106 (ebook) | DDC302—dc23/eng/20240808
LC record available at https://lccn.loc.gov/2024032772
LC ebook record available at https://lccn.loc.gov/2024032773

Dedicated to all people struggling to find and keep loving relationships.
May this book be of benefit.

Mātā pitu upatthānam
Puttadārassa sangaho
Anākulā ca kammantā
Etam mangala muttamam

Support for one's parents
Assistance to one's partner, children, and friends
Jobs that are not left unfinished: this is the highest blessing.

—The Buddha, translated by Ṭhānissaro Bhikkhu[1]

The Four Noble Truths

1. *Anguish is everywhere.*
2. *We desire permanent existence for ourselves and for our loved ones, and we desire to prove ourselves independent of others and superior to them. These desires conflict with the way things are: nothing abides, and everything and everyone depends upon everything and everyone else. This conflict causes our anguish, and we project this anguish on those we meet.*
3. *Release from anguish comes with the personal acknowledgment and resolve: we are here together very briefly, so let us accept reality fully and take care of one another while we can.*
4. *This acknowledgment and resolve are realized by following the Eightfold Path.*

—Roshi Robert Aitken[2]

CONTENTS

Acknowledgments

It's impossible to truly acknowledge all the beings involved in the creation of this work, because in some way, everyone I've ever encountered has contributed to it. I thank you all.

Without the generosity of the Buddhist community this book could not exist. Teachers from many traditions have shared their experience and wisdom with me, both personally and through their books and recordings. I'm especially grateful to Sharon Salzberg, Ven. Robina Courtin, Greg Scharf, Yongey Mingyur Rinpoche, Thrangu Rinpoche, John Makransky, and Roshi Merle Kodo Boyd. Thank you to Insight Meditation Society, Mindful Astoria, and the Maha-Sangha for always welcoming me.

I could not have completed this project without the encouragement of my dearest of dear ones, Lori Piechocki, who hasn't stopped believing in me since we were children. Thank you.

My gratitude to my family, especially my husband, Michael Davey, and my niece, Madeleine Piechocki-Cannet, for their patience and love. And Denise Lostumo, who's always in my heart.

I am grateful to many students and friends who offered me so much trust, interest, and kindness while I wrote this book, including Renee Bochman, Mona Chopra, Stephanie Seiler, and Craig Geller.

My sincere thanks to my agent, Steve Harris, for his confidence and enthusiasm, and to Jonathan Kurtz and the rest of the staff at Prometheus Books for their commitment to this project. And to Alice Peck whose talent and gifted editing guided the book.

Finally, this work is based on my understanding of the Buddhist teachings. I trust readers will recognize the intention of the book and the overall spirit in which it is shared and overlook any misinterpretations or inconsistencies due to my ignorance.

FOREWORD

I was very happy when Kimberly asked me to write the foreword to this book. It's a wonderful guide to deepening the connections we share with those we love the most. It also provides us with many ways that Buddhist practice can help us sensibly and kindly approach the relationship challenges we all encounter, with simple tools to help us cultivate patience, compassion, and equanimity.

Kimberly is a householder—a married woman with a family, living an ordinary, modern life in New York City, who also teaches and practices the Dharma. In this book she shares her personal experiences with her partner, family, and friends with honesty and authenticity. She shows us how these relationships offer us a special opportunity to improve our capacity for happiness and joy and gives us practical, Dharma-based exercises and meditations so we can do it, too.

Such is the power of Buddha's wisdom that, as we change our perceptions of ourselves and our place in the world, we also transform our relationships. This has certainly been my experience drawing on the same traditional techniques that Kimberly shares with such clarity and insight in this vividly relatable book.

May each one of us come to recognize the people in our lives as precious jewels for the unique opportunity they offer in cultivating our lovingkindness! And may all who read this book encounter fresh insights to transform our relationships in the most transcendent way!

—David Michie
The Dalai Lama's Cat series
and *Instant Karma: The Day It Happened*

INTRODUCTION

The odds of not meeting in this life are so great that every meeting is like a miracle. It's a wonder that we don't make love to every single person we meet.

—YOKO ONO[1]

I believe that happy relationships are possible—*for everyone.*

Even if you've been married for twenty years and your routine is boring and stressful; your mom has always been a help-resistant complainer; and your dearest friend moved across the country—all of us can create lasting and joyful connections with the people we care about the most. Using simple tools drawn from the Buddhist tradition, you can cultivate appreciation, set wise expectations, and create meaningful and intimate bonds of mutual support and kindness with your partner, family, and friends. I know it's possible because I did it, and you can too.

That's because our happiness isn't dependent on everything in our lives being perfect. In fact, we can experience financial struggles, job loss, grief, and illness and still have appreciation, delight, and gratitude for everyone in our life. We can create happiness by improving the quality of our attention, the depth of our compassion, and our willingness to repair ruptures and let go of resentments. That's why I wrote this book. I know from both personal experience and my work as a meditation teacher that creating happy and loving links with ourselves and with each other is not only achievable, but can be done with simple and easily learned practices. In this book, I share traditional meditations and exercises that anyone can do to show you how to cultivate your inherent qualities of mindfulness, kindness, patience, love, and wisdom and use them to feel closer and more content with your partner, parents, children, and friends.

Like some of you reading this, I was once skeptical that reliable and loving relationships would happen to me. I grew up in a chaotic home, with an alcoholic mother and an angry father. Both they and their families argued and yelled, held grudges for months if not years, and complained about one another often. They were rarely happy—because they didn't know how to be. I wish they'd had the tools I have now, because if they had been able to apply them, they'd understand that caring and respectful relationships—intimate, compassionate, empathetic, and vulnerable connections with the people close to us—are truly possible. As you'll see, everyone—including you—can learn and create the conditions for the people you love and yourself to thrive and feel heard and understood, as well for you to be the wise and loving partner, family member, and friend you've always wanted to be.

Because of this family history, I assumed that happy relationships were polite, free from confusion, and orderly, and as a young adult, I tried to create partnerships and friendships like this. But I was quickly disappointed. That's because contrary to what I believed, and what you might believe too, all relationships—even good ones—have arguments, misunderstandings, and hurt and include lots of emotions: love, joy, and ease, but also frustration, anger, sadness, and boredom. What makes relationships happy isn't an absence of conflict or difficult feelings, it's our ability to skillfully navigate them with openness, mindfulness, gentleness, and honest and appropriate communication.

I've participated in many healing modalities including psychotherapy, eye-movement desensitization and reprocessing (EMDR), cognitive behavioral therapy, Zero Balancing® (a gentle energy-equalizing bodywork technique), and yoga nidra. All of these therapies helped me gain insight into my habitual patterns and conditioned judgments and beliefs as well as improving my ability to relate and connect to others. But it wasn't until I began learning Buddhist meditations, tools, and contemplations that my capacity to connect with myself and the people closest to me transformed. These practices taught me how to meet myself and everyone else with wisdom and compassion, even when I make a mistake or someone hurts my feelings. And they can teach you too.

A PATH TO HEALING

Although I've included many different Buddhist principles and techniques in these pages, all are guided by the foundational principle of Buddhism—the Buddha's first teaching of the Four Noble Truths. These are four indisputable facts that apply to every human being:

First Noble Truth: All of us are suffering.

Second Noble Truth: Suffering has causes and it's not inevitable.

Third Noble Truth: We can be free from suffering.

Fourth Noble Truth: There are eight disciplines and behaviors we can develop to gain our freedom and end our suffering. These are called the Eightfold Path: wise speech, wise conduct or action, wise livelihood, wise mindfulness, wise concentration, wise effort, wise intention, and wise understanding.

You'll see that all the exercises and contemplations in the following chapters will help you develop proficiency in the Eightfold Path and will lead you to orient your speech and actions in ways that are useful, non-harming, and beneficial—for all your relationships. In particular, most of the meditations are based on mindfulness and lovingkindness practices. Mindfulness will improve your ability to pay attention, without judgment, to what is happening in and around you in the present moment. It's through mindfulness that you'll start to notice that the people in your life aren't who you think they are—they're much more than that. Our partners, children, and friends are just like us—good, bad, and everything in between. With mindfulness meditation, we can see who they really are, instead of idealizing their best qualities or only focusing on their negative behaviors. Lovingkindness, from the early Buddhist word *metta*, is the quality of wishing yourself and others happiness. It's sometimes translated as love, goodwill, or friendship, and it's a state of mind that doesn't require anything in return. All happy relationships depend on your capacity to generate lovingkindness—it's what enables you to love well and wisely.

YOU CAN DO IT

If you yearn to reconnect with the people you love, wish you could soften your heart to yourself, and want to recognize all of the obstacles you've developed that prevent you from experiencing joy, this book is for you. Through the practices I share here, I've learned to make time for my friendships and have more patience and appreciation for my spouse. I know how to set compassionate boundaries and let go of resentment with my family members. I'll show you the same simple and effective methods and techniques that I use, and I know you can use them too. With practice, you'll learn to meet the difficulty and struggle of misunderstandings, hard feelings, and even painful conflicts with openness and clarity and experience gratitude and ease with everyone in your life. You'll discover it's possible to stop catastrophizing, strategizing, and trying to control everything and everyone and relax into the moment-to-moment unfolding of life with compassion, clarity, and confidence.

It's important to for you to know that it wasn't easy for me to allow myself to have genuinely happy relationships, and it might be hard for you at first too. Like me, you might start out feeling fearful of getting too close, or you may feel mistrustful or unworthy of love. Or you could become fearful of losing the people close to you once you realize how important they are to you. That's what happened to me when I began writing this book. I noticed that as I realized the depth of my care for my loved ones and their care for me, I started to think, "I'll be devastated if we break up, change, or one of us dies." Each time I sat down at my computer to work, I felt anxious and fidgety. I finally sat down on a kitchen chair, closed my eyes, and brought my attention to my breath. I said to myself, "May I be at ease," and became aware that my chest was tight and my jaw clenched. I finally understood what was happening with me, and I walked into my husband's home office, and said, "I think I'm afraid to write about happiness, because what if it all ends?" He smiled, and in his matter-of-fact wise way, said, "Well, it will end whether you write this book or not."

He expressed perhaps the greatest truth of life—that everything is impermanent, including our closest and dearest relationships. Although that might seem terrible and sad—and it is—it's also poignant and beautiful. That's why the Buddha encouraged us to remember and acknowledge that change and loss are the nature of being human. He showed us how to accept it without aversion or denial but rather with wisdom, appreciation, and gladness. This book won't make you immune to the vicissitudes of life—but it will show you how to appreciate the delight of simply being alive with the people you love, without trying to change them or keep them the same forever.

NOTES ON THE PRACTICES

The practices in this book are adaptations of traditional meditations that I've learned through my Buddhist training. Their purpose is to help you connect with yourself and the people you love, develop insight into your habits and behavior, and ultimately recognize the open, kind, and wise person that you already are.

All the practices can be modified for anyone of any ability. If you can't walk, sit. If you can't sit, lie down. If you have asthma or breathing difficulties, use sound instead of breath to anchor you. There is no wrong way to meditate as long as you're present-centered, paying attention, and meeting yourself with kindness.

Although everything in this book is a suggestion, not a requirement, I encourage you to *not* skip the practices. In my experience, spending silent time alone with yourself in meditation is healing, calming, and transformative—*but only if you do it*. It can be hard at first—you might be fidgety or bored—and that's okay. It takes time to get accustomed to paying attention to yourself in a new way. Don't give up. I'm confident you can do it because it was hard for me at first too, but with time and practice I'm comfortable and at ease with meditation, even on days when my mind is frustrated, dull, or filled with fast-moving thoughts.

There are twenty-five practices in this book. You might not resonate with all of them and that's okay. Stay with those that seem to most easily steady your mind and open your heart. You're welcome to *mix and match* the practices too—all are effective for many situations, so if an exercise from the Family section is useful when you're with your partner, don't be afraid to use it.

Most importantly, be sure to trust your wisdom while you're practicing. If a meditation makes you feel anxious or overwhelmed, stop and try
again later. If you feel too tired to practice, take a nap. And if you're discouraged and want to quit, remember the reason you're reading this book
and learning mindfulness and lovingkindness: to take care of yourself and
the people you love with benevolence, skill, and compassion, through the
joys and the sorrows and everything in between.

SECTION I

HAPPY PARTNERSHIPS

CHAPTER ONE

Relationships Are Messy

You might be tempted to avoid the messiness of daily living for the tranquility of stillness and peacefulness. This of course would be an attachment to stillness, and like any strong attachment, it leads to delusion. It arrests development and short-circuits the cultivation of wisdom.

—JON KABAT-ZINN[1]

PSYCHOLOGISTS OFTEN SAY ADULTS WITH TROUBLED CHILDHOODS WILL likely have a deep need to be close to their partners, but with that comes an even deeper fear of being so connected. It means some of us will yearn for intimacy, but as soon as we experience it, we'll find a way to get out of it. This was true for me for a long time. I met and got involved with men who were decent, kind, and loving and really wanted me—only to find a reason to reject them and end the relationship. I preferred dating and even getting seriously involved with men who were deeply ambivalent about me, but I never understood why. I only knew that their ambivalence meant we would never get too close, so I never had to run away.

When I was in my thirties, I began a relationship with Mateo, a talented journalist who, like me, had never been married, loved cats and books, and lived just twenty blocks uptown from my apartment. He was considerate, polite, funny, and fair. When we ate meals together, we shared the cooking and cleanup duties, and we each paid our own way when we went out. We dated for nearly two years, and during that time,

I thought we had a perfect relationship because we rarely disagreed on anything and only had one argument.

Then he had to travel for a month for work. During that time, I hardly thought about him and he hardly thought about me. When he returned, our relationship felt like a deflated balloon and we both agreed it would be best to break up. I was puzzled that it ended because we didn't have any problems that I could see—we were companionable, shared similar values, found each other attractive and interesting. But I'd mistaken self-sufficiency for healthy independence and our shared interests for intimacy. The truth was that both of us were afraid to reveal our difficulties, confusion, or less-than-pleasant qualities to each other and were determined not to rely on or truly trust the other. I thought that by avoiding conflict, ignoring resentment, and keeping my emotions to myself, I could avoid a "messy" partnership. Instead, I was unable to truly connect—because happy and lasting relationships are complicated.

By the time I was forty, I'd only had a few relationships that lasted more than two years, and by this time, I'd embarked on an entirely new career. I was studying Buddhism and training to become a mindfulness teacher. I was beginning to write about my life and share my work on the internet. And I was becoming even more ambivalent about finding a partner. Where I had felt certain and at times desperate for a long-term, monogamous relationship, I now wondered if that was what I really wanted. But I could tell that my single life was too easy. There was no one to mirror me, challenge me, or reflect my blind spots. I realized that I needed to make a change if I wanted to grow: find a committed boyfriend and get married, or become a Buddhist nun—both ways would increase my self-knowledge, one through relationship with another, the other through a relationship with myself and a community.

I was studying at a Tibetan monastery in upstate New York and considering participating in their three-year meditation retreat when I met Mike. He'd been divorced for a few years and was also a meditator studying Zen Buddhism. He was different from most of the men I had dated: he was direct about his intention to be in a committed relationship, rather than just hanging out or being friends with benefits like so many of the other men I met on dating apps. When he explained what he was looking for, it made me realize that for a long time I'd been waiting to meet someone with whom I could fall in love. I thought it would come from them—when the *right* person came along, then I would want to marry, commit, love them. But Mike showed me that was a delusion. It had to come from *me*—I needed to begin with an intention to love, commit, and to become intimate. Then I could find a person who shared that intention and create a relationship together. We married a few years later. I'd like to say it was happily ever after, but sometimes it's not. In fact, in the aftermath of an early argument, Mike gently said to me, "Kim, we'll be as happy as we want to be." And he was right.

Because change is always possible, you can be as happy as you want to be too—but it takes time, insight, and energy. Maybe you're like me and you don't know how to be a good partner because no one has ever showed you how to do it. There's hope! I'm generally considerate and kind, but sometimes dismissive and defensive, and I've learned to soften that and you can too. Although I didn't really think it was possible, I've created a happy relationship using many tools and modalities, but it's been mindfulness and lovingkindness that have helped me the most. These practices enable me to truly listen to my partner, validate his experience, and empathize with his feelings, regardless of who is *right* or *wrong*. Our lives together and separately aren't perfect: my best friend died unexpectedly a few years ago, Mike's elderly mom needs a lot of care from him, and my income dwindled during the pandemic. All of these things have caused stress and struggle for our partnership, but we've learned that our happiness isn't based on circumstances outside ourselves. Rather, it's based on our intention to be truly loving, patient, and kind—through thick and thin, with each inhale and exhale.

I use the term partner, spouse, husband, and wife interchangeably in this section, which I wrote for anyone in a committed partnership with another person, whether you're married or not, and whatever your identity—straight, gay, lesbian, transgender, cisgender. If you're sharing your life with someone, you can learn to bring greater contentment to your relationship, no matter how hard it might seem. You can create strong bonds of patience and empathy with yourself and your partner to sustain a lasting and loving relationship. I know you can do this because I've done it, and I've taught many others to do it too, using the teachings and exercises in this section. Drawn from the Buddhist tradition, conventional Western therapeutic techniques, and from my own experience, these practices are powerful tools that you can learn and apply to transform and heal old struggles, create new habits, and open your heart to yourself and your partner.

> While reading this section of the book, make an intention to benefit and not harm yourself, your partner, or your relationship with your thoughts, words, or actions. You can even put your hand on your heart and say, "I vow to communicate clearly and act with kindness." You'll be surprised how powerful it can be to articulate your deepest and best motivation.

There are probably many things about your partner that you find annoying and frustrating, and you might believe they have to change for you to be happy. Meditation practice will show you that taking care of your feelings with kindness, communicating honestly, and approaching your partner with compassion even when they are angry, disagreeable, or unlikeable can transform a relationship whether they change or not. That doesn't mean you'll suddenly like it when they forget what time the kids' soccer practice starts although you've told them countless times, or become indifferent to their refusal to unload the dishwasher. Rather, it means you will be able to pause in these moments, feel your feelings, and choose how you want to respond. You'll learn that partnerships have moments of misunderstanding, miscommunication, and rupture—and you can meet them all with kindness, patience, and compassion for you both.

When my husband realized our relationship would come up in this book, he cautioned me not to portray the two of us as some sort of New Age, filtered, perfect couple. He asked me to be sure to let you know that even though our marriage is happy, loving, and strong, we still make mistakes, get confused, and say or do the wrong thing at times—and that's okay. In fact, weeks or even months can go by without a real rupture—a fight or hurt feelings or an insensitive remark—but we always remember that another one will happen, simply because we're human.

The next time you have difficulties with your partner, instead of feeling like you've failed or someone is in the wrong, remember that you can learn to be patient and trust in yourself and each other and use your wise actions and tools of mindfulness and lovingkindness to help you resolve your upset, calm your distress, and repair your relationship, time and time again.

Lovingkindness is only one of four kinds of love described in the Buddhist tradition. They're called the *Brahmaviharas* or the Four Immeasurables and include lovingkindness, compassion, appreciative joy, and equanimity. All of these types of love are boundless, indiscriminate, and unconditional; they're an endless resource we all possess within us. Unlike the transactional type of love that most of us are familiar with—"If you love me, I'll love you back"; or the desperate, desire-type of passionate love—"I want you badly" or "I love you so much I'll die without you," love in the Buddhist tradition isn't transactional or conditional on anything or anyone. It's a simple gift from your heart that truly wants for you and the people you care about to enjoy an abiding sense of ease and well-being.

The first immeasurable, *metta* or lovingkindness, is a simple wish for another's happiness and an expression of the kind of contentment that isn't dependent on getting what you want but rather being glad for what you have. The second immeasurable of love is *karuna* or compassion; this is your natural inclination to empathize with another's suffering and to do your best to alleviate it. You've experienced compassion anytime you've felt the impulse to reach out to someone who is struggling with illness or grief. The third type of love is sympathetic joy or *mudita*, and this is when you feel glad for someone else's good fortune. It's the way you express love for a family when their baby is born, or when someone you care about gets a promotion. And finally, the fourth expression of love is *upek-kha* or equanimity, the balance and steady-mindedness you experience when you know you can't stop someone you care about from suffering or making bad decisions but you choose to stay patient and kind without trying to control them or fix their circumstances.

Practice One: Let Yourself Love

Like too many of us, I believed for a long time that love was something someone else needed to give me, and when they did, I would feel at ease, relaxed, and happy about myself. I assumed that I would find it within romantic relationships, so I searched for a boyfriend or partner. But even when I was in relationship with kind, compassionate people, I still didn't feel very good, and I wondered why I wasn't getting the love I needed.

It wasn't until after I started studying Buddhism that I began to believe that love doesn't come from other people at all. I finally understood that it's a quality that I already possess, and you do too. After I committed to a regular mindfulness and lovingkindness practice, I began to experience a pervasive sense of "okayness"—a feeling of well-being no matter what was happening good or bad in my life. This feeling isn't reliant on someone else or the result of success, money, or praise. I'm confident you can discover this inner resource too, and with practice you'll realize that you have all the love you need. Though at times it might be obscured by conditioning and old habits, remember that you can always rely on it and access it whenever you get still and quiet.

If you're feeling lonely or unwanted right now, or waiting for someone else to give you the love you believe is missing from your life, please try the following meditation. Practice it daily for at least six weeks and observe how it unfolds in your mind and your heart.

1. Find a quiet and comfortable place where you can relax for at least fifteen minutes. You can sit in your favorite chair, lie down on the couch with a blanket, or rest on your porch with your dog. Put all of your devices out of reach.

2. First, don't do anything at all. Just let yourself get still. Then take a few deep exhales and full inhales. Do this for at least five minutes.

3. Put your hand on your chest, and say silently, *May I be open to all the love in my heart.* Just keep repeating this phrase to yourself. You don't have to feel warm and fuzzy or anything at all. But when you get distracted, don't let yourself get caught in stories or arguments with yourself. Just gently notice and come back and begin saying the phrase again.

4. After five or ten minutes (or longer), think of a dear friend who is self-critical. Imagine they are sitting here with you. Then silently say to them, *May you be open to all the love in your heart.*

5. Next, connect with both yourself and your friend's presence. Keep your hand on your chest and say to both of you, *May we be open to all the love in our hearts.*

6. Finally, let yourself rest quietly here for at least one minute, without saying the phrases. Then slowly and mindfully choose to open your eyes, stretch or move, and thank yourself for your beautiful heart.

Chapter Two

The Sweet Life

It is entirely possible to create new, mindful, positive habits. This is certainly attainable with the practice of loving speech and deep listening toward ourselves. Positivity and gratitude slowly become a new, mindful habit.

—Sister Dang Nghiem[1]

For many years, Roger wanted to find a partner, fall in love, and get married. He truly believed that if and when it happened, he'd feel completely different about himself—satisfied, happy, and confident. So he dated many women and even asked one to marry him, but none of his relationships worked out . . . until he met Clare. They matched on a dating app, and he thought she was amazing as soon as he met her. They dated for a few years and when Clare unexpectedly got pregnant, they were both delighted and spontaneously got married at the courthouse and celebrated with a joyful dinner for friends and family. Roger was thrilled. He had everything he wanted, and when his daughter was born, he was euphoric. But within a few years, he felt the same way he did before he met Clare—not exactly unhappy, but mildly dissatisfied, disappointed, and a little bored.

One of the reasons I wrote this book was because I used to feel this way too. I believed my ordinary and mundane life and relationships were missing something special. Before, and even after I got married, I was always planning for a trip or a special entertainment to look forward to, because unless something new, shocking, or exciting was happening, I was bored. In fact, I thought that being discontent or disappointed with regular life was normal, and you might think this too because so many messages from our culture suggest we need to have more and be better to be happy. But this is a lie—nothing has to change for us to feel satisfied with our life; we just need to pay attention to what we already have.

In the First Noble Truth the Buddha recognized that no one is immune from suffering or *dukkha*—the universal, moment-to-moment dissatisfaction or sense that something is missing or not quite right about our relationships or ourselves. We often think of suffering as something terrible and tragic, but *dukkha* also includes the kind of suffering that causes us to feel like Roger, or to think that if our partner changed or if we moved into a new house, we'd feel better than we do right now. But the source of your suffering isn't your spouse or circumstances, it's your relationship with yourself. That's why mindfulness is so transformative, and why one Buddhist word for mindfulness, *sati*, means to remember or to recollect. Because that's what happens when you bring your awareness to the reality of the present moment—you apprehend clearly all that you have and how beautiful it is. Instead of believing the stories in your mind about how your life and relationships *should* be and everything that's missing from them, you can develop awareness of what is actually present with mindful attention. Try it now: shift your focus away from what you think you don't have or what you don't like about your partner or your life and become aware of what you really *do* have—your many resources, your own wisdom and clarity and other positive qualities, and all the wonderful blessings of your relationships.

This doesn't mean that my—or your—life and partnerships are perfect, or that you should ignore your partner's destructive habits or behaviors like addiction, rage, or deceit. On the contrary, when you choose to practice mindful attention and let go of the fantasies and delusions about how you think your life should be, you'll be more likely to see the reality of your situation with clarity. If there are serious problems, you'll be able to awaken to them and approach them with sensitivity and care for yourself and your partner.

But, if you're like me, you'll likely discover there aren't any insurmountable difficulties with your spouse. You'll notice that you have a pretty nice life, that your partner is a reliable, caring, and patient person, or that they are funny, generous, and adore you, or that they're supportive, intelligent, and good. And once you become aware of these truths, you'll notice what you have (so much!) and feel gratitude for your life, your marriage, and yourself. This is the beginning of *sukha*—the opposite of *dukkha*. *Sukha* means "sweetness," and you'll feel it infuse your heart and mind as you pay attention to your blessings and appreciate them. Living a sweet life means being at ease and content with what is, meeting difficulty without denial or blame, and receiving and acknowledging the gifts and resources of your life and relationships.

If you feel bored with your partner or think you know everything there is to know about them, take a minute to pay closer attention. Put away your devices, turn off the television, and take a breath. Let yourself observe and notice this person as they are, right now, without your story about them. Speak silently and say to them, "I appreciate your beauty and kindness."

As your appreciation arises naturally through mindfulness, the dullness or boredom of familiarity for your partner will ease. When it does, I hope you'll share your newfound sense of gratitude with them. Appreciation is among the easiest ways to create happiness and joy, and I know from experience that sharing your gratitude for your spouse *with* your spouse can transform *dukkha* into *sukha*—because I've experienced it many times, and I imagine you have too, if you stop to think about it. It happened to my husband and me recently when I had to meet a deadline for work. I was busy all day and teaching meditation classes at night, and I hardly had time to contribute to the household. I didn't help much with the cleaning and laundry, and instead of cooking, Mike and I ordered dinner from our local Chinese restaurant several times a week. He was supportive, but after two weeks or so he asked me—very kindly—when

I thought we could spend time together. I shook my head in anger. I felt misunderstood: Couldn't he see how hard I was working? Didn't he understand that I was doing my best? I went back to my office and before I opened my laptop, I took a deep breath. I realized that Mike was feeling a little lonely and taken for granted, and I understood why—I was being a bit too self-absorbed and inconsiderate. I really did appreciate his patience and his encouragement and unwavering support, so I went back to the living room and apologized, and we made plans to spend the next morning together. It was Sunday and I cooked a Dutch pancake for breakfast, and as he poured milk into his coffee cup, I told him that I knew it wasn't easy to live with me right now, that I was grateful for his generously and kindness, and that I felt lucky for our relationship and all he brings to it. He smiled and I reached across the table and held his hand. We have a sweet life together and I was glad to remember that and share it with him.

I hope you'll also remember to share your sincere and simple thankfulness with your partner too. It will make them—and you—feel seen, heard, loved, and valued.

You likely tend to use the word *love* a lot, like "I'm madly in love with them" or "I love those shoes," but what you really mean is you have an attraction, a want, or a yearning to possess something or someone. In Buddhism this is called *attachment* or desirous love, and it's often confused with lovingkindness or *metta*. The first of the Four Immeasurables is a powerful force of goodwill, given freely without obligation, and it's not transactional. When you truly love your partner you're not trying to possess them or get something from them. Rather, your love bestows goodwill and happiness to them, and it helps both of you thrive, flourish, and create harmony with each other, your other relationships, your community, and the world. This kind of true love can be developed and cultivated with attention and practice, and I hope you'll use the exercises in the book to do it. You might be surprised to discover—like I did—that your capacity to care about your spouse can increase—not decrease—over time. The satisfaction and joy you can feel for each other is unlimited and boundless, achieved through practice, intention, and effort.

Practice Two: Counting Your Blessings

It's so easy to get caught up in all the things you don't like or that annoy you about your partner, so it's important to take time to focus on what you appreciate and enjoy about them. Try this simple exercise to help you cultivate a sense of gratitude and gladness for your spouse and your marriage. When you practice this regularly, you might be surprised by the long list of blessings that you discover if you pay attention. It will encourage you to develop gratitude for your partner, and I hope you'll consider doing it together with them and sharing your notes with each other like one of my students and her wife do. They write their gratitude list every day on sticky notes and post them on the wall above their bed, and now they have a tangible and beautiful reminder of their happiness to support them whenever they look at it. You can also modify this exercise to include everything you're grateful for—your own good qualities, material goods, resources—as well as your partner, family, and friends.

In addition, I encourage you to keep a Gratitude Journal, where you write a list of your gladness every day. I note mine in an inexpensive grid-lined notebook, and each morning I sit at my desk with my colored felt-tipped markers and jot down three things I appreciate, love, and am grateful for. Recent entries include my niece Madeleine, fresh tomatoes, and the NYC Department of Sanitation for picking up our garbage. I try not to enter the same item twice, and this forces me to pay closer attention to things I might otherwise overlook, like access to medical care or my favorite running shorts.

1. Find a quiet spot where you can be undisturbed for fifteen minutes. Have a pen and a notebook or Post-it Notes within reach. Sit down, close your eyes, and put your hand on your heart and on your belly. Rest here and don't get up, feeling the movement of your body as you breathe. Stay and relax in your presence for five minutes.

2. With your eyes still closed, imagine three things your partner said or did in the past few weeks that you enjoyed, appreciated, or feel grateful for. It could be the meals they cooked for you, the moments when they listened and responded to your requests, or their financial generosity to your life together. Then, open your eyes and write them down.

3. Close your eyes again and ask yourself, "Did I miss anything? Is there anything else I appreciate about my partner?" Whatever arises, go ahead and write it down too.

4. You can set aside your pen and paper; close your eyes for a few minutes and allow yourself to feel appreciation for your relationship. Silently say to your spouse "thank you" or envision light from your heart radiating to their heart.

5. Finally, take a few minutes to feel appreciation for yourself. Silently say "thank you" to yourself before you conclude this exercise.

6. Repeat daily.

CHAPTER THREE

Creating a Refuge

When there is love, there is no duty. When you love your spouse, you share everything with them—your property, your trouble, your anxiety, your joy. You do not dominate. When there is love, the word duty disappears.

—J. KRISHNAMURTI[1]

TWO YEARS AFTER DAVID AND LESLEY GOT MARRIED, DAVID LOST HIS job. He was a manager at a popular seafood restaurant that abruptly closed because of the owner's tax problems and mismanagement. David and Lesley felt lucky; with a little budgeting and belt-tightening, they and their children were fine with just Lesley's salary as an executive assistant. But David was ashamed and embarrassed as he looked for a new position. He felt like a freeloader, and when Lesley got home from work in the evening, David would make sure he was busy—baking bread with the kids, painting the sunroom, or scrubbing the bathroom cabinets. One day, Lesley came home to find David napping on the couch with a sore throat. As soon as he noticed Lesley, he jumped up, scurried to the kitchen, and started preparing dinner. Lesley followed him and gently said, "David, I just want you to know this is your home. You don't have to earn your place here." As he reached for the onions, David put down his knife and began to cry.

Living in a stable and comfortable home, where we feel relaxed, safe, and able to be ourselves, can help us heal old wounds and trauma and inspire a sense of deep contentment and trust in our marriage and each other. For some people—including me—this isn't an easy task. If your past was turbulent, like mine was, you might believe you have to do something special to deserve love, like prove your value by performing tasks or providing financial support—or that you must hide your weaknesses and flaws for fear you'll be spurned or belittled. But don't worry; if you feel this way in your relationship, it's still possible to create a *refuge* for your spouse and you—a shared home, where you both feel loved, heard, supported, and secure, no matter the circumstances.

The next time you're at home relaxing with your partner, reading a book, watching television, cooking dinner, or doing anything else that's part of your mundane and ordinary routine, I'd like you to stop and just take a moment to notice it. Put your hand on your heart and say silently, "May we be safe and happy."

I learned about the idea of refuge through my Buddhist training. It's an important aspect of the tradition, which offers acceptance and safety to all Buddhists. It began when the Buddha was alive, and he taught everyone who wanted to learn from him, regardless of social status, ethnicity, or sex. He didn't require allegiance, payment, or an examination. He didn't judge their looks, background, or aptitude. A person only needed to ask, "May I take refuge with you and your community?" and he would respond, "Welcome." That's because the Buddha understood that all humans have the ability and potential to develop our hearts and minds, but we require a place of safety and support from which to do it. Buddhists still offer refuge to anyone who asks, and I encourage you to do the same for you and your partner. You can create a sanctuary where both of you can be vulnerable and honest and easily reveal your worries, jealousies, and insecurities to each other, knowing you won't be judged, snubbed, or mocked.

You can create a refuge no matter where you live (a house in the suburbs, a small, rented apartment in the city, or even if you're staying at your parents' home) because in the Buddhist tradition, refuge includes physical and spiritual dimensions, representing both a location and a mind-state of safety and sustenance where you can find protection, guidance, and peace in the face of life's challenges and uncertainties. Creating a refuge together means that you regard each other as the most important person in your lives, that you recognize and appreciate that you both have beautiful qualities, and that you're willing to accept each other's imperfections and shortcomings, without contempt, pity, or condescension.

I've talked to so many people who've been married for years who are open and patient with their partner's struggles but still can't truly relax or believe they are completely accepted by their spouse. My former boss Jacqui told me that her boyfriend, Mitch, hasn't seen her without makeup in the six years they've been living together, because she thinks she has to be "pretty" for him or he might leave her for someone else. And Danny, who was on crutches when we met at a meditation retreat, said he was embarrassed to allow his husband to take care of him when he broke his leg. He decided to recuperate at his mother's house because he knew she wouldn't think he was disgusting or unlovable—but he wasn't sure of his spouse. If you feel this way in your relationship, I encourage you to develop awareness and lovingkindness for the secret insecurities that make you feel unworthy of being loved. Then you can communicate your worries to your partner. A true refuge includes mutual understanding and openness to help you alleviate one another's doubts and shame. This will deepen your bond and dismantle the barriers and defenses between you that prevent you from receiving love and trusting your partnership unreservedly.

I really struggled with this, and sometimes I still do. If, like me, your childhood home was not a safe place for you, you're probably feeling the same way. I spent a lot of time in my room alone, reading a book and trying to take up as little space as possible so my parents wouldn't notice and criticize me. When I grew up, I was very comfortable living alone but never at ease when I was with other people. In college when I was living with roommates, I didn't eat dinner in the kitchen or watch movies in the living room with the others, preferring to be by myself in my bedroom. But when I finally got my own apartment, I truly found my first real refuge. There I was safe and comfortable and relaxed, and it was such a relief to finally not worry about being yelled at for accidentally breaking a glass or harassed for sleeping past ten. Years later, when I moved in with my now-husband, I was surprised that I had the same impulse to hide and the same worries about being judged that I'd had when I was a child. I thought these feelings had gone away, but in our Brooklyn apartment I was always watching Mike to make sure he was okay with me and wondering if I should do something—cook, make a joke, or please him in some way, to prevent him from getting angry or annoyed with me. I found excuses to go to bed early and read by myself because I wasn't comfortable relaxing on the couch "doing nothing." But Mike noticed my discomfort. He encouraged me to relax and reminded me that I was safe and that this was my home, too. I slowly learned to let him know when I felt worried or insecure and he was happy to reassure me. A few years later, in a new place we purchased together, he returned from a Knicks game to discover me tucked under a blanket on the couch in pajamas, watching a Hallmark Channel holiday movie and eating popcorn, a cat snuggled on each side of me. He could tell that I finally felt at home and at ease, and he sat down near me and smiled and said happily, "My work here is done."

Buddhists take refuge in what we call the Triple Gem: the Buddha, the Dharma, and the Sangha. Here, *Buddha* means both the original Buddha who is our inspiration, as well as the open and wise metaphorical Buddha that resides in our minds and hearts. *Dharma* refers both to the Buddhist teachings and the Truth—that life and all phenomena are impermanent and constantly changing, that cause and effect are real, and that our greed, hatred and delusion cause us suffering. And *sangha* means community—both the Buddhist monastics and students, as well as the larger community of spiritual seekers like ourselves, in all traditions, striving to awaken to our wisdom and compassion.

Taking refuge isn't a test of devotion to the Buddha or to any of the Buddhist sects but rather a commitment to yourself to release what's not valuable and to rely on what really matters in life—your connection to yourself and the world, and your kindness, love, good sense, compassion and all your other beautiful qualities. That's why the Buddha, Dharma, and Sangha are called the Triple Gem— because they're priceless and valuable treasures we can all rely upon. Although some Buddhists take refuge in a formal ceremony like I did, where a Tibetan Rinpoche (respected teacher) welcomed me to the sangha, cut a lock of my hair, recited blessings over me, and gave me a Buddhist dharma name (Tenzin Dolma), refuge doesn't have to be bestowed upon you by another person. You can do as countless Buddhists have done for centuries: simply repeat these Refuge Vows three times to yourself every day as a reminder of what really matters in life:

"I take refuge in the Buddha, my own open and wise nature."

"I take refuge in the Dharma, activities that lead me to recognize my open and wise nature."

"I take refuge in the Sangha, those who support me in finding my open and wise nature."

Practice Three: Coming Home

Buddhism encourages all of us to discover our wise, stable, clear mind, so we don't have to look to other people or material possessions to make us feel satisfied, loved, and happy. This is often described as our "true home"—a centered, grounded, and spacious sense of consciousness that you can take refuge in. This exercise is designed to help you and your partner discover your true home, in yourself and in each other. It's especially beneficial if you feel unsettled or insecure in your relationship and you want to create a safe and welcoming sanctuary for yourself and your partner. You can practice it alone or with your spouse.

1. Sit or lie down somewhere quiet. Put your hand on your heart and inhale deeply and exhale fully. Rest your attention on your palms, heartbeat, and breath for five minutes. If you get distracted by thoughts, let go of them and return to the sensations of your body.

2. Keeping your hand on your heart and your attention on the movement of your breath, connect with your own loving presence. You can imagine you're looking at yourself in a mirror. Then say these words silently, *I take refuge in my true home; I take refuge in activities that lead me to recognize my true home, and I take refuge with my partner [Name] to discover our true home together.* Repeat for at least five minutes.

3. Next, connect with your partner. Imagine them sitting near you or feel their presence, and say to them silently, *May you take refuge in your true home; may you take refuge in activities that lead you to recognize your true home, and may you take refuge with me to discover our true home together.* Repeat for a few minutes.

4. Finally, imagine both of you together. Maybe you visualize that your partner is here with you even if they're not. If they are with you,

hold their hand. Feel your love for each other, and silently say, *May we take refuge in our true home; may we take refuge in activities that lead us to recognize our true home, and may we take refuge and discover our true home together.*

CHAPTER FOUR

When You're So Mad

With understanding, you can restore peace and harmony in yourself and in your relationships with others. You will know how to act and how to react with intelligence so that you are no longer in a war zone, a zone of conflict. If there is peace and harmony in you, the other person will recognize it, and peace and harmony between both of you will be restored quickly.

—THICH NHAT HANH[1]

WHEN SARITA'S NEW CUPCAKE SHOP BECAME POPULAR, SHE HAPPILY worked for many hours a day, even on weekends. But this made her wife, Charlie—who wholeheartedly believed in Sarita's dream to open her own bakery—angry. She didn't understand why Sarita now spent little time at home, and even when she was there, she was thinking, planning, or talking about counter help, cake design, or the price of flour. When Charlie shared her frustration and told Sarita she hadn't anticipated how much the store would change their life, Sarita became defensive and accused Charlie of being unsupportive. Charlie, feeling unheard and mis-understood, called Sarita selfish, and Sarita, hurt, shut down and refused to speak to her. She began to spend more time at the bakery, and Charlie grew increasingly resentful.

Sound familiar? That's because it is. Although no relationship is entirely free from conflict because no two people will always share the same views, want the same things, or concur on everything, you might not have been taught or know how to work through anger or the hurt feelings that arise from disagreements. In fact, you might indulge your upset like Charlie or get defensive and avoid arguments like Sarita, which can further damage or even ruin your closeness and intimacy with your partner. That's why, if you want to have a happy marriage or partnership, you'll need to make space for disputes and learn to have healthy conflicts. And that begins by understanding how to manage your anger with patience, mindfulness, and lovingkindness, so it doesn't destroy or injure you or your spouse.

From a Buddhist standpoint, getting mad or having anger isn't bad or immoral. But if you let it escalate, it will grow into hostility and aggression, and that's when you'll cause harm with your words and actions. This is why the traditional Buddhist teachings instruct us to care for *ourselves* when we're angry—to pay attention to what's happening in our bodies, minds, and hearts, with patience, skill, and grace.

When frustration arises, you might have a habit of fueling it with resentful thoughts like "He always does this" or "I'll never get what I need." I've done this many times, especially when I'm sure I'm right, because then I think my anger is understandable. When you notice that you're believing that you have a justified reason to be angry, it's a sign to stop and take care of yourself. If you rationalize your upset feelings, it means you're suffering and confused, and if you continue to let your irritation fester, you'll destroy your peace of mind, your goodwill for your spouse, and your ability to think clearly. That's because a desire for vindication (being told your view is right or that you win) won't help you feel less hurt or upset. The only way you'll feel better is when you feel heard, empathized with, and understood—by you.

This is true even—or especially—if you're someone who doesn't like to have anger toward your spouse, and instead of feeling justified in your resentment, you feel guilty or ashamed of it. You may have been taught that having hard feelings about someone you love means you're an awful person, and if so, you probably try to deny or hide your frustrations. If this is your habit, it's likely one of two things will result: you'll feel depressed or upset with yourself, or you'll reveal it to your partner in passive-aggressive remarks or behaviors. That's what Charles did to his wife, Karla, for a long time. When he got upset with her, he would grab his keys from the table, stand up, and say, "I'm going to the gym." The result was that Charles had difficulty getting his needs met and his wife felt abandoned.

> While it's normal for spouses to disagree, get mad, or feel resent-ment, it's not normal to inflict or endure destructive speech or actions. If you or your partner is aggressive, enraged, and/or cruel with words or behaviors—using degrading or insulting speech, or violence—it's a sign to take a time-out. Stop talking and leave the room or the house and stay away until both of you have calmed down. If your partner is abusive, you should consider leaving the relationship. In the Buddhist tradition, true wisdom means that you don't cause harm, and you don't let anyone cause harm to you. If you suspect you're suffering from domestic abuse, please contact the National Domestic Violence Hotline at 800–799-SAFE. They're available 24 hours a day, 7 days a week.

Caring for yourself when you're furious, outraged, or indignant means deeply listening to your body, spirit, and mind. First, make space for physical sensations like a racing heart, sweaty palms, or stomach distress—and deeply inhale into you discomfort and fully exhale with an audible sigh. Take time to empathize with your stress by placing your hand on your heart and saying silently, "This is a painful moment." Now you're ready to explore the content of your thoughts. Are you ruminating on old grievances or making a list of all the ways your partner hurt you before? If so, gently stop. Bring your attention to your torso, deeply inhale and fully exhale, and say to yourself again, "This is a painful moment." Repeat these methods as needed, using your patience to stay still and silent.

Remember—it's important to wait until you feel calmer before reen-gaging with your spouse. Conflicts can't be resolved when either of you are reacting out of pain or anger because it will create more division and misunderstanding. Instead, take your time to calm down, even if it means waiting to reconnect for a few hours or even days. And just because *you* feel ready to talk again, doesn't mean your partner will be. You'll have to check in with them and gently ask if they're available to reengage with you. If they say no, don't get offended—use your patience to steady your mind and remember you're both suffering right now. When you each feel you can be receptive to your own and your mate's emotions, then you can restore communication. You'll know you're ready when you appreciate that you're both on the same side again, even though you still feel hurt or view things differently.

It's hard to practice with anger because it has so much energy and power. You'll probably get caught in it again and again, and that's okay, it happens to me too. Just keep trying because over time you'll increase your capacity to be with the discomfort of it, just like I have. People tend to assume that because I'm a Buddhist teacher and a meditator I'm always soft-spoken, reasonable, and patient, that I'm never swept away by frustration, or that my marriage must be tranquil and calm. But that couldn't be further from the truth. When I feel dismissed or think my husband is utterly wrong, I feel hurt and angry just like you. Sometimes I still react badly, shouting, interrupting him, or walking away in annoyance, because I don't feel heard or understood. But thanks to my training, my anger doesn't last as long as it once did. Now I know how to bring patience and attention to my distress, listen to my upset, and offer compassion to my pain and confusion. I often do walking meditation—silently pacing back and forth in the hallway. Other times I sit on a bench in my kitchen and drink a cup of tea silently. I know you can learn to do this too. You can make friends with your distress, bring steadiness to your body, and soften your mind no matter how upset you feel . . . again and again.

There are many Buddhist stories about anger, but one that feels especially close to me is about the fierce bandit, Angulimala. He was the leader of a cruel and violent gang that robbed and murdered their victims, and his name means "finger necklace" in the Pali language because he wore a collar made from the hands of the people he'd killed. Many of the villagers were terrified of him, so one day they asked the Buddha for his help, and the Buddha went into the forest to search for Angulimala. The Buddha's students begged him not to go because they thought he was no match for this strong, fierce, and brutal man. But the Buddha wasn't frightened or worried, and when he found Angulimala and his henchmen, he calmly asked Angulimala to stop inflicting pain and suffering on the local people. This enraged Angulimala and he ran after the Buddha, intending to kill him. But the Buddha walked away. Magically, though Angulimala was swiftly chasing him, he couldn't catch up to the Buddha. Angulimala screamed in fury, "Buddha stop!" but the Buddha kept walking ahead of him. When Angulimala had chased the Buddha for miles and still not caught him, he demanded again that the Buddha stop. But this time the Buddha turned to this violent man and said fiercely, "I stopped a long time ago! Now you stop, Angulimala!" Exhausted from his rage, Angulimala collapsed and suddenly understood that his hatred was causing him tremendous suffering. He realized that he could stop hating and destroying, just like the Buddha had stopped his own hateful thoughts and destructive behaviors. Angulimala bowed to the Buddha right there in the forest. He surrendered his anger and became one of the Buddha's most accomplished and wise students.

Although I'm not a thief or a violent person like Angulimala, and I doubt you are either, I sometimes share his confusion, temper, and upset. I have moments of feeling disconnected from my love, kindness, and compassion just like he did, and maybe you do too sometimes. If you know how painful it is to feel enraged and hurt, you'll also know how powerful and healing it is for someone like the Buddha—a teacher, therapist, good friend, partner—to listen to your struggle, share with you the means and tools to help yourself, and give you the confidence to be free. Like Angulimala, you and I can surrender our hostilities and find peace, time and time again.

Practice Four: Welcome Anger

Many of my students insist that their anger is useful, and they're suspicious about letting go of it. They worry that if they have less fury, they'll be indifferent to injustice or hurt, or they'll allow others to take advantage of them. But the truth is that destructive anger—when you're feeling malicious, hostile, or demanding things go your way—is never useful. It might make you feel as though you're powerful, but you're really just confused and likely to make reckless decisions. This kind of anger also masks vulnerable feelings like heartbreak and sadness and disconnects you from yourself. So the best way to work with the force and painful sensations that arise when you're enraged is to not avoid it or try to discharge it on others. Instead, you can reconnect with yourself and welcome your anger and treat it with lovingkindness and compassion. When you're able to acknowledge your pain, comfort your distress, and calm your thoughts, your anger will transform into wisdom—clarity and good sense—so when you see injustice and hurt you'll be able to take useful actions that lead to peace and understanding, for yourself and the world.

1. Sit or lie down in a quiet place. Put your hand on your heart and just notice what's happening—without judgment. Feel places of warmth, tightness, coolness. Notice your breath and the sounds around you.

2. Sense what is happening that tells you anger is present. You might feel sweaty palms, shakiness, or shortness of breath. Or maybe your throat or chest are tight and constricted. Or maybe you have mean and spiteful and racing thoughts.

3. The next time you breathe in, put your hand on your heart and inhale all of these symptoms of anger. Breathe in your upset feelings and sensations as though you're welcoming an old friend. Make each exhale long and steady.

4. Continue for several minutes.

5. Before you end this exercise, say to yourself silently, *May my anger, upset, and confusion be transformed into compassion and wisdom.*

6. Repeat as necessary.

CHAPTER FIVE

Change and Transitions

Everything that has a beginning has an ending. Make your peace with that and all will be well.

—JACK KORNFIELD[1]

WHEN JAMES TOLD THERESA HE WAS GOING TO LEARN TO PLAY TENNIS, she laughed. They'd been married for several decades, their kids were in college, and in that entire time, Theresa had never seen James work out or participate in sports. He was relatively fit and watched his diet, and since they had retired they liked to walk together on the weekends. When the kids were younger, they hiked as a family, but she couldn't imagine him playing tennis—it just wasn't *him*. She could tell James was hurt by her response, and she tried to sound encouraging, but she really doubted he could do it and was surprised that he wanted to.

George and Sarah had lived together for only two years, but both felt they were each other's soulmate. That is, until they moved to Chicago—a decision they made together because they both wanted to live in a bigger city—and their entire relationship seemed to unravel in less than a month. Sarah discovered she didn't like living in an apartment and yearned for their old backyard and the quiet of a smaller town. George was disappointed that Sarah wasn't more resilient, adventurous, and able to enjoy the differences and let go of the past so they could explore their new home together. Soon they were considering splitting up.

Like both couples, my husband and I mostly live happily and peacefully together—until something or someone changes. If you're in a partnership, you'll recognize the unsteadiness that the unexpected creates in your relationships. Whether it's good or bad, change will unsettle one of you or both of you, and if it's big enough, it can cause a rupture, retreat, or grave misunderstanding. That's because—whether it's planned, imposed, or just surprising—new experiences and transitions are hard. They force us to acknowledge our expectations about ourselves, our partners, and our future, and often require us to change, too.

> When you and your partner are dealing with change—whether it's happy, sad, or neither—before you say or do anything, first be sure you're connected to each other. Literally reach out to your partner by taking their hand, putting your palm on their shoulder, or hugging them. If you're not together in the same place, then text them or call them with supportive words, like "I appreciate you" or "I'm glad we're together in this." Then take a breath as you say to yourself silently, "May we both be at ease and happy."

When I anticipate all the changes that are happening now and bound to occur later (What if Mike or I get sick? What will happen if we don't plan well enough for retirement?), I feel overwhelmed and scared. The Buddha recognized this as a particular type of suffering—*viparinama-dukkha*, which means the suffering of change. Even though I know that aging, sickness, and death are unavoidable and will happen to me just like they'll happen to everyone else, I don't want to accept it and insist on trying to find an escape route. But the Buddhist teachings insist that we remember the nature of life is always in transition and flux. The cherry trees blossom and fade. The baby becomes a toddler. The new couch wears thin, afternoon becomes evening. Everything—external circumstances, natural phenomena, our thoughts and moods and bodies—is inevitably and constantly shifting and impermanent.

Buddhism understands that learning to accept and even welcome change is the antidote for the suffering of change and the upset it brings and the key to a peaceful and balanced life. Using its tools—following the Eightfold Path and practicing lovingkindness and mindfulness—will help you let go of any anger, denial, or disappointment you might feel when things shift and transform. They'll help you open your heart to new circumstances and meet them with openness and grace. And remember, it doesn't matter if you like what's happening or not! What's important is that you stop resisting it, so you can deal with it appropriately—with kindness and insight. Even if the change is painful or hard, you can say yes to it and bring peace to your mind and heart.

If you feel disturbed by changes in your partner or their reaction to changes in your life together, it might be because their reaction challenges your idea of who they are or should be. When a story or belief we hold is contradicted, like it was with Theresa about James, you can feel like you're losing the person you know and love and that can be scary. But it can also be an opportunity for learning, growth, and deeper intimacy. Perhaps your view of your partner is too narrow and inflexible; if so, you can learn to include more aspects of who they are and help them feel understood and appreciated. Perhaps you're hurt that they can't see the possibilities within challenges; if so, you can bring lovingkindness to your feelings and share them honestly with your spouse. My husband and I have discovered that when we're in a transitional time (caused by a change in employment, a kitchen renovation, or even just traveling to a new place), we need to sit down on the couch together and practice mindful breathing before we speak or discuss what's happening. This way, instead of trying to control each other, the unfolding of life, and countless circumstances which aren't up to us, we can focus our energy on what we *can* change: our own minds, and the way we speak and treat each other.

The Eight Worldly Winds is an early Buddhist teaching that describes four opposing conditions—gain and loss, fame and disrepute, praise and blame, joy and sorrow—that everyone will experience, no matter who we are or what our circumstances might be. One day we might get a job we like, only to be fired a few years later. In the morning our spouse might praise our cooking, yet in the evening our daughter tells us the meal we made for dinner is awful. The Eight Worldly Winds is a reminder of an undeniable fact: everything will change whether we want it to or not.

Most of us try to create positive circumstances where we feel good and avoid negative situations that make us feel bad. This strategy would be wonderful except we don't have control over everything and everyone. The truth is, happy moments will always end and difficult encounters will always arise—it's not up to us. That's why the Buddha encourages us to train our mind and heart so we're steady no matter what is happening, and that's the meaning of the Eight Worldly Winds. You can experience your joy and your pain without desperately trying to keep the former after it ends, or avoiding the latter through shame, blame, and disbelief. When you buy a new house, you can keep your mind confident and appreciative of it. When you lose it in foreclosure a few years later, you can keep your mind confident and appreciative too—that you have your health, family, and other resources. That's because even though losing your home is sad and hard—and you'll do your best to make sure it doesn't happen!—it doesn't have to destroy your kindness and good sense. You can rely on your strong and spacious heart and mind to hold your sorrows and your blessings as they come and go, with wisdom and compassion for yourself and everyone else.

Practice Five: Trust in Change

The Buddha tells us that you need trust, diligence, and wisdom to thrive despite the ever-changing and impermanent conditions of your life. Trust means developing a deep and abiding confidence that you won't be devastated even when something awful happens. Diligence is your determination to stay mindful and steady even when you're excited or hurt. And wisdom is keeping your good sense and clear-seeing so you're not chasing pleasure, surprised by pain, or bored with dullness.

You can develop these qualities with the following exercise. It combines mindfulness of physical sensations with lovingkindness meditation, and I hope you'll practice it whenever you're unsettled by unwelcome surprises or resistant to new ideas.

1. Notice when you feel unsettled by changing circumstances and before you say or do anything, choose to sit down somewhere quiet where you can be undisturbed.

2. Set a timer for ten minutes and commit to staying there until the alert sounds.

3. Put your hand on your heart and scan your body. Start at the top of your head and slowly become aware of your face, your neck, your torso, arms, seat, legs, and finally, your feet.

4. Feel the sensation of your breath from the tip of your nose to your navel.

5. Imagine a person you care about—it could be your spouse, a family member, or a friend. As you see their face and envision that they're seated next to you, say to this person, *May you trust yourself to meet the unfolding of life with kindness and wisdom.* Say this phrase silently, again and again, as if you're giving them a gift.

6. Continue to imagine this person sitting next to you. Notice their care and sincere concern for you and your well-being. Hear them say to you, *May you trust yourself to meet the unfolding of life with kindness and wisdom.* Just for a few minutes, allow yourself to hear them repeat these words to you. Let yourself receive their good wishes, and let their blessings wash over you.

7. Now you can imagine that you are offering your blessings to both of you. Say silently, *May we trust ourselves to meet the unfolding of life with kindness and wisdom.*

8. When the timer rings, don't get up right away. Take a moment to sit silently, then thank yourself for your efforts before you resume your activities.

CHAPTER SIX

Resentments and Forgiveness

If you let go a little, you will have a little peace. If you let go a lot, you will have a lot of peace. And if you let go completely, you will have complete peace.

—AJAHN CHAH[1]

WHEN MEGAN, JAYLEN'S WIFE OF NEARLY TWO DECADES, TURNED FORTY, he planned a big surprise party for her. He rented a room in their favorite restaurant, ordered a buttercream cake from her favorite bakery, and invited her closest friends and family, even contacting old college friends, months in advance so they would have time to make travel arrangements. But a few weeks before the event, Megan's sister told her about it, and instead of feeling happy and grateful as Jaylen expected, Megan accused him of intentionally giving her a gift she would never want—a surprise. He had to admit she was right; he knew she didn't like surprises, but he'd truly thought for such a special occasion she'd enjoy it. He apologized and offered to cancel it, but Megan decided to go ahead with it. When the day came, she enjoyed seeing her loved ones and felt glad for the celebration, but she was still annoyed at Jaylen. That was seven years ago, and at least once a year, Megan brings it up during a dispute or an argument as evidence of Jaylen's inconsiderate nature and his stubborn refusal to put her needs above his sometimes.

Resentment and hurt arise from not feeling heard, understood, or acknowledged by your partners *and* yourself. Sometimes your hurt seems petty or stupid and you just want it to go away, or sometimes your partner is unable to tolerate your pain and responds indifferently or wonders why you just can't get over it. You might be thinking that happy couples simply *shouldn't* cause harm, but it's unavoidable at times, because everyone makes mistakes. I've been with my husband for many years, and we still hurt each other sometimes, through ignorance, misunderstanding, and inattention. What makes our relationship successful—and can make your relationship successful as well—is that we've learned to mitigate the damage we cause, repair it, and most importantly, *let it go*. We do this by stopping our rumination over our hurt so we're not stuck in a cycle of grievance and withholding out of meanness or spite.

Clinging to a sense of being wronged or injured isn't a sin and it doesn't make you a bad person, and letting it go is not something you *should* do for your spouse's sake. Rather, it's something you should do for yourself. The old saying "Resentment is like taking poison and waiting for the other person to die" is true. If you tightly grasp your resentment and perceived (or real) ill-treatment, the person most affected will ultimately be you.

Some things are too big to let go of easily. Deceit, betrayal, and abuse can't and shouldn't be simply forgotten or forgiven unless and until they are addressed, amends are made, and meaningful change occurs. Be careful not to accept (or make) any apology that doesn't clearly express regret and acknowledgment of words or actions that caused harm. "I'm sorry you feel that way" isn't enough—it doesn't take responsibility for one's behavior or express an understanding of the effect of one's actions.

For a long time, I thought letting go of the past, especially difficult moments, would make me stupid and cause me to repeat the same mistakes and let others, especially my spouse, take advantage of me. But Buddhism helped me understand that it's possible—and even desirable—to forgive *but not to forget*. Forgiveness means letting go of hard feelings that are painful, and if you choose to do it, you're not agreeing that you were wrong, that the other person caused no harm, that you're okay about what happened, or that it didn't happen at all. What you're saying is that you've decided that it's not useful for you to keep holding on to the past, that you accept that your partner makes mistakes and has limitations just as you do, and that you're willing to let go of the action so you can begin again.

I also used to believe that if my husband really loved me, he would easily and quickly let go of his resentment because he knew I didn't really mean to injure him or I had a good excuse for doing it. That's because admitting even to myself that I'd caused him pain made me feel like an awful person. You might believe this too, but you can learn—as I have— that offering yourself kindness and forgiveness will help you accept *your* mistakes and repair them, too. You don't have to defend yourself to your partner or explain to them why you did what you did; you just need to validate their feelings, empathize with them, and sincerely apologize, without blame or shame.

One of the reasons Megan continued to talk about the surprise party that she didn't want was because Jaylen never really acknowledged why she was hurt. He just said that he didn't mean to upset her, really wanted her to have a great birthday, and was sorry if she didn't want the party. When he finally said, "You're right, I know you hate surprises and I'm sorry I didn't remember and consider that. I understand why you got upset," she felt understood and seen in a way she hadn't before, which led to her relief and lessened resentment, ultimately reducing the conflict.

Living intimately with another person means that sometimes you'll have to let go of the annoyances and frustrations you have about your partner again and again—and that's okay. Instead of feeling outraged because they won't change, you can feel friendship and even humor toward their irritating habits or imperfections, especially if they're not meaningful or your thoughts are unkind. It took Kerry a long time to realize this, because every night, for years, his partner, Rabhi, took off his socks in the living room and left them on the couch or the rug and it made Kerry mad. Because Kerry hated untidiness, he bent down and picked up the socks whenever Rabhi left them there. Kerry took them to the hamper, feeling humiliated and annoyed. One night he angrily shouted and demanded that Rabhi stop leaving his socks all over the place, to which Rabhi shouted back, "I've told you a hundred times to stop picking them up! When I'm done with work I just want to relax and not worry about little things. I'll pick them up in the morning." Kerry finally realized it was his own anxiety that was making a big problem out of nothing. Socks on the floor overnight wouldn't hurt anyone, and true to his word, Rabhi picks up his socks and takes them to the hamper most mornings. And each night when Rabhi turns on the NBA game and unconsciously slips off his socks and drops them as he stretches out on the couch, Kerry cringes . . . and then smiles.

In Buddhism, *sankappa* or intention, is the underlying motivation that drives our speech, behavior, and even our thoughts. Everything we do is directed by our intention, which is why Wise Intention is one of the disciplines on the Eightfold Path. Psychologist and meditation teacher Sylvia Boorstein describes it as "the guide that points us in the right direction and brings us back on course when we lose our way."[2]

Wise Intention can be developed and refined through meditation and mindfulness, and unlike a goal, it's not about creating a specific outcome but rather reorienting your moment-to-moment actions toward the good. An easy way to do this is to just remember why you want to do something, because doing so strengthens your intention. You can say to yourself, "My intention for being married is because I want to take care of my spouse and me," "I intend to play basketball to stay healthy and connected to my friends," or "I'm reading this book to help my family heal." Instead of using a specific intention, you can also use the vast motivation followed by many Buddhists: "All my actions are intended to benefit and not-harm all living creatures." And that includes you!

Practice Six: An Intention to Let Go

Sometimes it's incredibly hard to release something your spouse said or did that caused you pain, even though they apologized for it with sincerity, acknowledged their mistake, and validated your feelings. This practice will help you bring compassion to your experience and make an intention to let go, even if it isn't possible for you to do so just yet.

1. Find a comfortable seat where you can be silent and undisturbed for the next fifteen minutes or so. You can sit or lie down. Move your devices out of reach and commit to being present without distraction for the entire time.

2. First, don't do anything at all—just relax and breathe for a minute or two.

3. Place one hand on your heart and the other on your belly. Let them rest there as you feel your presence and trust that you are here for you. Notice how your belly rises as you inhale and how it contracts as you exhale. Consciously and deliberately breathe deeply five times.

4. Now, connect with your hurt. Where do you feel it in your body? What thoughts are arising? Let yourself directly experience these sensations and ideas without creating a story or judgment about them.

5. Continue connecting with this painful experience. Use deep breathing and keep your hand on your heart and on your belly if you feel overwhelmed. You can say to yourself about your feelings, *It's okay to be here*. Reassure yourself by saying this or any other comforting words. Repeat to yourself, silently or audibly.

6. Now say to yourself, *When I'm ready, I will let go of this painful experience*. Repeat a few times.

7. Finally, imagine you and your spouse together in a moment of happiness and connection. Say silently, *May we remember our love and kindness for each other*. Repeat for a few minutes.

8. Stop saying the phrases and simply rest your attention on your natural breath and the palms of your hands. Repeat as often as necessary.

CHAPTER SEVEN

Trauma: The Past Is Present

Our 25 years together have not been a fairytale. We had four years
that were pure hell. We went to couples therapy and it helped a lot.
He was always willing to work at it. Because after that first burst of
falling in love, inevitably every relationship has moments where you
have to decide: is this worth my time?

—Nicole Ansari-Cox[1]

WHEN I WAS A CHILD, MY FATHER OFTEN BECAME ENRAGED FOR WHAT seemed like no reason at all. If my mom forgot to pick up the dry cleaning or if I said I didn't want to eat dinner at home that night, he could explode. The fury arose so fast—one minute we were talking about going to visit my grandparents, the next instant he was screaming that no one could hear him and why wouldn't anyone listen to him? If we tried to respond or engage with him, he just yelled louder, so for a long time when he acted like this, my mom and I would stare at him silently, frozen and afraid, waiting for him to stop. But years later, his second wife, Jean, wasn't scared of his rants and responded differently to him. When he started yelling at her, she would say calmly, "Jim, I know you're upset that your mother didn't give you what you needed, but I'm not your mother. Stop screaming so we can talk about this." To my surprise, it often (although not always) calmed him down enough to share his feelings with her— which were disproportionate to the matter at hand but were still very real to him. Jean understood something my mother and I hadn't—that my dad's rage wasn't really about the dry cleaning or anything we said or did; it was about his childhood trauma from the death of his father when he was five years old and his upbringing with a mother who neglected and emotionally abused his brother and him.

So many of us are like my dad—we've had painful, traumatic childhoods that impact all our relationships, but especially our partnerships. When we become intimate and close with another person, it feels like a familial situation, and family, for those who've experienced a traumatic childhood, is a dangerous and unsafe place to be. Fear, anxiety, rage, or a need to flee might arise from a seemingly mundane interaction like your wife unexpectedly coming home late from work. But just as your childhood trauma was caused by other people, so too can your trauma be healed *with* other people. Relational wounds are mended through healthy relationships, and you and your partner can use mindfulness, patience, and kindness to slow down your difficult interactions, identify when the past is influencing the present, and learn to help instead of hurting each other.

Emotional or physical abuse or abandonment and neglect are among the most common traumatic situations from our past that can endure in our bodies and minds and unknowingly affect our relationships with our current partners. You or your spouse might be struggling with unresolved complex trauma if you

- Repeatedly have a strong negative reaction or feeling that doesn't make sense.
- Experience bad feelings as familiar and common, and you've felt this way since childhood.
- Often feel a sense of danger or panic, although there is no cause for it.
- Distrust your spouse without reason, viewing them as an "enemy" or against you.
- Believe that others can't hear you, understand you, help you or ease your pain.

If these statements are true, you or your partner could be struggling with complex post-traumatic stress disorder (C-PTSD). C-PTSD is the result of repetitive or prolonged emotional or physical distress or abuse, and it generally includes a sense of helplessness and lack of agency because the mistreatment often occurs when the person is powerless—as a child, or a victim of domestic abuse, war, or trafficking. If you suspect C-PTSD is affecting you or someone you love, it's important to address this with individual professional treatment. Find a trauma-informed psychotherapist who can offer you evidence-based treatments such as cognitive behavioral therapy, Somatic Experiencing®, or eye-movement desensitization and reprocessing (EMDR).

If you've noticed particular times when you or your partner have powerful responses that don't seem to make sense or are inconsistent with the situation at hand, you might be reliving unresolved traumatic events from your past. The loss of a parent or sibling, physical or emotional abuse, accidents and injuries—all of these can impact us deeply and for a long time. When something occurs in the present that reawakens this wound from the past, it can cause us to react as if the past were happening all over again, and we might respond by feeling terror, shutting down, or becoming angry and enraged.

For years I struggled with my own experience of childhood trauma, which mainly manifested as panic attacks. I felt frustrated by them and wanted them to just go away. I blamed my parents and family and wondered why they didn't realize how much their actions hurt me, and I also felt ashamed. I thought there must be something wrong with me because I couldn't seem to "get over it." You or your partner might feel this way too, and I encourage you seek support. I worked with a compassionate therapist who helped me understand and process my past, so it operates less powerfully in me today, here in the present. Meditation practice has also contributed to my healing, and I hope you'll try this too. Learning to be still and sit quietly was uncomfortable at first, but gradually I became accustomed to the sensations of my body, and this significantly eased my anxiety. Now I feel much more open and confident that I can experience even the most unsettling feelings of fright and fear without being over-whelmed—and you can too. You can develop a spacious sense of being that can hold all your experiences with compassion, so you don't need to reject, blame, or dread any feeling, even panic attacks.

That's what happened to Candace. Her husband, Dan, noticed she was anxious every time they left home for a trip. It didn't matter if it was just an overnight visit to her mom's house for Thanksgiving or a long-anticipated vacation in Belize; if they planned to travel, Candace was unusually affected by it. It started before they even left their house; she would stay up late obsessively cleaning, sorting through the hall closet or removing all the books from the shelves and dusting every inch. In the morning, exhausted from lack of sleep, she would be short-tempered and impatient, repeatedly going over her packing list and telling everyone what to do. Whatever excitement Dan and their kids were feeling was destroyed by her mood, and he began to dread going on vacation.

Dan and the family were happy and looking forward to their trips and couldn't understand why Candace didn't feel the same way. It didn't make sense . . . until they went to therapy together. There, Candace revealed that every time she left home, she had a terror that it would not be there when she returned. She imagined a fire burning the house down, a disaster preventing her from ever coming back, or even someone else moving in and locking them out. She knew it was absurd and yet the fear and panic she felt was real, overwhelming, and powerful—and the same feeling she'd had when she was a kid, taken from her beloved grandmother's house to the chaos and neglect of her parents' apartment, over and over again.

Candace began individual therapy with a woman who specialized in helping people with traumatic childhoods, and she also enrolled in a mind-fulness based stress reduction (MBSR) program. Now, when she starts to feel the familiar distress before traveling, she sits quietly in the kitchen and counts her breath instead of frantically cleaning. And Dan is more patient with her and doesn't dismiss her worries and tell her they're ridiculous. Instead, he reminds her that if the worst does happen—if, for some unfore-seen and inexplicable reason, they lose their home when they're away, they can trust themselves and each other to create a new one together.

The third type of love from the Four Immeasurables, *karuna* or compassion, is a profound wish for everyone to be free from suffering and the causes of suffering. Compassion transforms pity, indifference, and disgust into understanding and empathy. With compassion, you can truly connect with your struggles and pain and offer your beautiful presence to anyone you know who is tormented with trauma or anguished by grief. As one of the immeasurable qualities, compassion is indiscriminate and boundless: that means it doesn't discern between friends or enemies or *good* and *bad* people or actions. The power of compassion recognizes that everyone—even dangerous people—are just the same as you are: helpless in the face of sickness, injury, and loss and deserving of compassion, empathy, and care. You can see why Buddhists consider compassion to be among the greatest forces in the universe.

Practice Seven: Be with Your Body

Your body is your original home and yet you might be disconnected from its needs and sensations. If you are, you run the risk of losing your connection to the truth because, unlike your brain, your body is anchored in the present moment where reality exists and where we can apprehend it through our senses. That's why many teachers describe the feeling of being steady and in tune with the present as being *grounded*—in contact with your breath, sound, smell, taste, sound, touch, and the earth.

If you're experiencing unsettling, disturbing, or painful thoughts, images, memories, or feelings in your body, it's harder to stay connected to it. You might notice you're daydreaming or fantasizing because you want to escape this uncomfortable and upsetting experience. The next time this happens to you, I hope you'll do the following practice. It doesn't matter if you know the source of your upset or not because *why* you're feeling this way doesn't matter right now, but *what* you're feeling does. Instead of playing a video game, watching a movie, having a drink, or any other unskillful coping mechanism you've been using to distract yourself, try this first. The most important thing right now is that you turn your attention to your discomfort with kindness and love, instead of trying to avoid it.

1. Stretch and move! Take a few minutes to reach your arms above your head, bend over (releasing your knees) and let your arms stretch to your toes, gently roll your head, and stretch your neck. Stand up and shake out your right leg, then your left. Lift your left foot and balance on your right leg, then reverse. Do any movement that feels appropriate and useful to you right now.

2. Next lie down flat on the floor on your back. Let your arms relax next to your torso, and your feet rest in whatever position is natural. Use a blanket if it's too hard or cold, but try not to use a pillow.

3. Place one hand on your heart and one hand on your belly. Feel your breath from your navel to your nose. Notice how your hands move with each inhale and exhale, too.

4. Count your breath backward from nine. The first full breath (one inhale and one exhale) is *nine*. The next full breath is *eight*. Continue counting until you get to one, then start again at nine. Don't force or strain—just allow your body to breathe naturally. If you miss a breath or get mixed up on the count, start again at nine. Remember, this is not a contest and you can't get it wrong. Just keep gently starting again as needed.

5. You don't have to avoid painful or difficult emotions. If they arise, you can note them and acknowledge them by tenderly saying *I see you*, then gently return to counting your breath.

6. Continue this exercise for ten minutes. It's most useful if you do it frequently—a few times a day—for short periods of time. You can even set an hourly alarm and practice for five minutes each time it rings.

Chapter Eight

Spiritual Partners

Being responsible for my actions,
I shall free myself and you.
Will you free me, too?

—Sensei Wendy Egyoku[1]

John heard shouting and ran out of his home office to find his wife, Geeta, at the kitchen table with her phone in her hand, sobbing. She'd just had another argument with her oldest daughter, Lila, a sophomore away at college who she thought was making foolish decisions, as evidenced by her C average and the amount of time she spent with her friends. Although Geeta kept telling herself not to get angry and not to raise her voice, she was so scared and impatient that she called Lila stupid and selfish. Lila said nothing and hung up the phone and Geeta knew she'd really hurt her daughter's feelings. John sat down next to his wife and rubbed her back as she cried, and when she was able to speak, she told him what happened and how bad she felt about it. He told her it was okay to make a mistake and that she should call her daughter when she was calmer and apologize. He also said, "I know you can do better because I've experienced how patient and loving you are, and I'm confident you can learn to manage your anger."

Whatever your faith, tradition, or religion (or lack thereof), being in a committed relationship with another person is a unique opportunity to bring out the best in each other. I think of this as a *spiritual partnership*—a relationship that fosters and encourages you to recognize and manifest the most beautiful qualities of the heart. Being part of a couple offers you a unique opportunity to know another person in a deeply intimate way. You get to witness their public, private, and even secret selves—an honor few other people, if any, will ever experience. You can use this gift of intimacy and knowledge with care and insight to help your partner see how beautiful they are, encourage their positive traits, and gently discourage habits that lead them to struggle, hurt, or feel bad about themselves. In Buddhism, a person who does this is called a *kalyanamitra*—a spiritual friend who gently helps guide us toward love, compassion, and wisdom, leads us away from the poisonous mind-states of greed, hatred, and stupidity, and reflects back to us our clarity, kindness, and skillful actions.

> One of the best ways to create a spiritual relationship is to spend time together in silence. Go for a walk or have dinner at home without talking, reading, watching television, or looking at the internet. Spend a few hours doing household chores like laundry, dishes, and cleaning without using words, or sit together silently and pray or meditate.

If you'd like to be a *kalyanamitra* for your spouse (or your friends and family), you'll need to commit to your own personal practice of mindfulness, lovingkindness, and nonharming speech and actions. That's because a spiritual friend isn't a judge, critic or instructor, nor are they in a superior position, bestowing their wisdom from a lofty seat. As a spiritual friend, you are a peer, standing alongside the people you love, guiding them gently as you walk together on the path of compassion and wisdom. Rather than pointing out your partner's flaws, foibles, and mistakes, your job is be a mirror and reveal to them their courage, talent, and generosity and all their other beautiful qualities, and allow them to do the same for you.

Although you might believe that if you push yourself, your partners, your kids, or employees to be their "best" by scrutinizing their "problems" and reprimanding their "bad" behavior, both psychological research and common sense show us this is rarely effective. While it often causes people to work harder in the short term, in the long term it creates shame, self-doubt, and low self-esteem. When you inspire people through positive reinforcement, they're more likely to learn to behave with kindness, diligence, and good sense, and you are too.

This is how dolphins are trained. Like humans, they're intelligent and sensitive creatures, and they don't learn through punishment or force. So when a dolphin performs a requested behavior, their trainers reward them with treats and praise. But if they don't perform as asked—or do something else—their trainers ignore it. This is how the dolphin learns to focus on the positive behaviors it's encouraged to do. You can approach your partner in the same way. Be mindful of your reaction the next time they make a mistake or say something you think is embarrassing or unhealthy. Instead of replying with frustration or annoyance, you can choose to say nothing. Alternatively, be sure to use positive reinforcement the next time your spouse makes an appointment with their dentist or doesn't get impatient with you when you forget to take out the garbage. Be sure to tell them you notice and appreciate it.

As a spiritual friend, you must model the behaviors that will help you and your partner flourish. This means to treat yourself the same way you want your partner to treat you—with kindness, respect, and care. Be sure to speak and act toward yourself with gentleness and consideration, because it's impossible to expect your partner to be patient with themself if you're always finding fault with yourself. If you criticize them for eating junk food or for ruminating on things over which they have no control when you do it too, they won't learn from you. When you release self-blame, become conscientious about eating well, or manage your stress appropriately, it will generally have a positive influence on your partner too.

Remember, sometimes being a spiritual friend doesn't require you to *do* anything—it's meaningful just to give your wise, receptive, and open presence to your partner and allow yourself to receive theirs. A few years ago, when my nonprofit job was ending due to lack of funding, I felt unsteady and concerned about what would happen in the future: how would I make money, could I earn enough as a meditation teacher to make a living, and would this change harm my marriage? But when Mike and I discussed what was happening, he remained steady, calm, and non-reactive, so I did too. We were able to navigate a challenging time with clarity and kindness for each other, despite the stress of uncertainty and a change in our finances, and you can do the same.

If you want to create a spiritual partnership, it can help to have the support of community, too. In Buddhism this is called a sangha. A sangha is a group of people who believe in the importance of wisdom, caring, and respect for living beings and who help each other reinforce these values in their hearts and minds. Your sangha could be with a local meditation group, a neighborhood volunteer program, or at a church, temple, or mosque. You can even create a sangha of two with your partner. Make a commitment to each other to encourage, inspire, and honor your deepest principles and strive to help each other be the best person you can be.

You might be surprised to learn how significant spiritual relationships and communities are in the Buddhist tradition because meditation and contemplation seem like solitary endeavors. But the Buddha recognized that people who are kind, sensible, and loving influence others in a profoundly positive way, strengthening their best qualities. He also noticed that people who are cruel, greedy, and selfish influence others in a profoundly negative way, intensifying their worst qualities. So he encourages you to seek out people who can help you with your spiritual growth and avoid those who hinder it. He explained this in a beloved teaching he gave shortly before he died, called *Half the Spiritual Life*. In it, he emphasizes that being with wise, kind, and loving people is not just half or a portion of the spiritual path, but rather our relationships with these people are actually the entirety of spiritual life. To illuminate this, the late Korean Zen teacher Seung Sahn used to tell his students a metaphor. He said that their training together was similar to cooking many potatoes in a big pot with little water. Just as the crowded potatoes bump into each other as they boil and knock the dirt off one another, good people living and working closely together get the same results.[2]

Practice Eight: How to Build a Spiritual Partnership

These five actions are clear guidelines you can follow to become an effective *kalyananmitra*—spiritual friend—for your spouse and for yourself. They're practical and easy ways to help you foster a strong and intimate connection and create a loving and safe environment where you both can thrive and flourish. I hope you'll practice them together with your partner.

1. Don't give advice. Learn to listen and be patient with your partner instead of trying to fix their problems or tell them what to do. If they're struggling, your willingness to be present and receptive to their feelings is helpful and healing. Only give suggestions when directly asked to do so. If you're not sure what to do, you can ask them, "Do you want to be heard, helped, or hugged?" and respect their answer.

2. Show appreciation. Maybe the easiest and most joyful way to connect with and reassure the people we care about is to remember and notice their good qualities and what we like about them and then tell them. It lets your partner know they are loved and valued.

3. Give people space. Space doesn't mean distance or ignoring anyone—it simply means to allow your spouse to experience their feelings or challenges in their own way and at their own pace. If you're like me, you might find it hard to tolerate your partner's upset feelings and try to make them feel better. But their feelings aren't up to you and if you notice you have an impulse to approach them too soon, it means it's time to sit quietly with yourself and become mindful of your distress and comfort it.

4. Stay steady and calm. Emotions such as anxiety or worry are contagious, and if you're able to authentically keep a steady mind and an open heart, you'll help your spouse feel confident and less fearful, even during an unsettling time.

5. Learn to take pleasure in silence. Talking isn't the only way to develop a strong relationship or even to communicate. Sitting together silently, taking a quiet walk, or choosing to just listen without speaking can help create a relationship of trust, openness, and joy.

CHAPTER NINE

Sickness, Loss, and Grief

When we're with somebody who's sick, try and tune in to see what it is they need. Because often they need something really practical. And sometimes they need something spiritual. Sometimes they need material things. And so, to try and tune in, rather than go in with an agenda.

—VENERABLE THUBTEN CHODRON[1]

FOR NEARLY A YEAR, DIANA HAD BEEN URGING HER HUSBAND, CHRIS, to see a doctor about an unusual brown spot on his back. When he finally did and he was diagnosed with skin cancer, Diana was irate. For several weeks she could hardly speak to her husband because she felt he should have listened to her and visited a doctor much sooner. She resented him for putting himself and their family in an uncertain situation. But her anger made Chris feel alone and hurt, and even after she calmed down, he only grudgingly would accept her help and comfort. At a time when they needed each other the most, they were unable to connect because they could not release their resentment, frustration, and blame toward each other.

There's a reason old-fashioned wedding vows include the commitment to stay together *for better and for worse, in sickness and in health.* That's because no matter how young or old or how rich or poor, all couples will encounter illness, injury, or disease—because it's part of the reality of being human.

61

If you're like me, you probably have a hard time truly accepting this. You might believe a delusion that you share with many: that if you're careful about what you eat and you exercise and get regular checkups, refrain from dangerous activities like skydiving and taking heroin, and always cross with the light, then you—and people you love—won't catch a cold, break a collarbone, have a stroke or a heart attack, get cancer, or struggle with arthritis. But as much as you and I don't want to believe it, this delusion is demonstrably untrue. You do not know anyone who has not caught a virus, had an infection, or pulled a muscle. As a living creature, it's impossible to utterly avoid illness, disease, injury, or accident.

You might hate to accept this reality because it makes you feel helpless and vulnerable when you prefer to feel that you're in control and powerful. If this is true for you, you might find yourself getting angry or finding ways to place blame when you or someone you love is unwell. But when this happens, you're forgetting that sickness is not a judgment or an indicator that someone did something wrong—it's simply the poignant result of being a fragile and impermanent human being. That's what Diana didn't want to accept, and fortunately for her, her sister told Diana she was behaving badly because she was afraid. Diana recognized she was right; underneath her exasperation she was terrified that Chris would become debilitated or die. She realized she needed to take care of her fearful emotions because they were preventing her from caring for her husband and family.

The next time your partner or you are sick or injured, remember that you're not alone. Whatever you're facing, there are many other people who share your experience. Put your hand on your heart and say to yourself silently, "May all of us who are [struggling with heart disease/in the ICU/dealing with long Covid/have a broken leg] be healed, recover easily, and be free from physical and mental suffering." Repeat this silently whenever you feel overwhelmed or wonder "Why me?"

When your partner is sick, you have a choice: let illness or injury bring you closer or let it push you apart. If you choose the former, you'll need to be honest with yourself about your feelings, so you can be honest with your partner too. It's important to know what's really happening inside your mind and heart, because if your vulnerabilities and fears are driving you, you will act unwisely. To prevent this from happening, you can use mindfulness and lovingkindness to soothe and steady yourself, to stay present-focused, tune into your partner's needs, and get clear about the reality of the situation. Then you'll be able to respond in ways that are supportive, helpful, and healing.

I feel upset and anxious when I can't protect my husband from physical suffering, and it took me a long time to learn to manage these feelings. I learned to focus my attention away from his needs and toward my own discomfort—so I can tolerate his pain with openness and patience and wisdom. Then I can do my best to ease his struggles with a compassionate and loving presence instead of giving advice or trying to control things. I say to myself, "Kim, don't just do something, stand there," and at times it's really hard! For example, when Mike tells me his back hurts, my first instinct is to tell him to go for a run or do a stretch or ask him if he'd like me to massage it for him or bring him an aspirin. This makes him feel annoyed and frustrated and unheard—because he doesn't want me to *do* anything at all. Is this familiar to you? If so, that's because we all want our partners to understand and empathize with our pain instead of trying to make it go away, because that's not possible. Rather than trying to control something out of your control, you can help your partner feel cared for and loved by deeply listening and validating their experience. These days, when I notice I'm trying to take charge of my husband's physical or mental health, I stop talking, take a deep breath, and put my hand on my heart. I experience how difficult it is for me to allow him to be unhappy, in pain, or challenged—because it feels like it's my responsibility to fix him or take his pain away.

I was pretty disappointed, and maybe you will be too, when I discovered that no matter how hard I study and practice Buddhism and meditation, it won't make me indifferent to sickness, aging, or even death. I wished that mindfulness and lovingkindness practice would protect me from negative feelings, especially in the worst moments. But this isn't possible or even desirable—because we need to feel empathy, sadness, and even pain sometimes, in order to stay connected to ourselves and each other. That's what compassion means. It's the opposite of indifference or avoidance, and when you have compassion, you'll stop trying to care less or push away negative feelings and circumstances. Instead, you'll use your kindness and good sense, and all your other beautiful qualities, to make wise decisions that will contribute to healing, preventing harm, and creating healthy conditions for yourself and the people you love.

When Diana began to identify and bring compassion to her fears about Chris's diagnosis, she stopped blaming either of them for it. She knew that the real explanation for Chris's cancer was simple: he was human and sometimes humans get cancer. She felt a new sense of appreciation for their relationship, realized how important he was to her, and told him so. This helped him forgive her, and they both developed a deep sense of empathy for each other's struggles. Diana was able to be more skillful in what she said and did, and Chris was able to be more patient with her, knowing she was struggling too. There were still moments when Diana got angry, tried to tell the doctors what to do, or felt she needed to take control of the treatment plan. But she remembered to come back to herself, again and again, and when she noticed tension in her shoulders, an upset stomach, or her racing heart, she recognized these as symptoms of being worried and afraid, put her hand on her chest, welcomed all that was arising in her heart, and reminded herself that she didn't need to do anything at all in that moment except breathe.

When I began to study Buddhism, my teachers encouraged me to remember that I—and all of us—will grow older, get sick, die, and lose what we love. I thought this was a gloomy and somewhat pessimistic outlook. I didn't understand why we had to emphasize it and think about it all the time. But after months of daily contemplation of the Buddha's Five Remembrances, I was surprised that I felt more at ease with these truths, and as a result, I also felt more appreciative of my health, life, and the people I care about. From the *Upajjhatthana Sutta* [Subjects for Contemplation], they remind us that nothing is more important than remembering and embracing the true nature of life. I hope you'll recite them daily to help you feel less surprised by impermanence and change and more grateful for your partner and the time you have together. I printed them out and framed them and they're hanging above my desk so I see them often. Maybe you'll consider doing the same.

The Five Remembrances

1. I am of the nature to get sick; I can't avoid sickness or injury.

2. I'm of the nature to age; I can't avoid getting older.

3. I'm of the nature to die; I can't avoid dying.

4. Everyone I know and love is of the nature to change; I can't avoid losing everyone and everything I love.

5. My thoughts, speech, and actions are my only true possessions; I can choose to use them to benefit or I can use them carelessly and cause harm. Either way, I will be affected by the outcome.

Practice Nine: Facing Uncertainty

If you and your partner are experiencing uncertain and distressing events, it's easy to get caught up in worry about what will happen to you in the future. Maybe you're afraid of serious illness as you await the results of medical tests, fearful of a divorce or separation after discovering a betrayal, or you're dreading the possibility of financial stress if you or your partner lose your job. You might find that you're imagining a wonderful outcome and moments later envisioning the worst. If so, I encourage you to try this exercise to help you let go of both hope and fear and meet the uncertainty of the moment with clarity, openness, and good sense.

1. Sit or lie down in a place where you won't be disturbed. Close your eyes, get still, and take five deep breaths.

2. As you inhale, imagine you're breathing in all your worries and hopes.

3. As you exhale, imagine you're breathing out calm, clarity, and peace.

4. When you breathe in, say to yourself, *Inhaling fear, worry, hope, desperation.* You can also imagine your difficulties as a cloud of dark smoke that you draw into your heart.

5. When you breathe out, say to yourself, *Exhaling calm, ease, peace, okayness.* You can also imagine the smoke you inhaled is transformed into a bright golden light that you release through your nose.

6. If you like, you can include other people in this meditation. Imagine you're inhaling the fears and hopes of your partner, and as you exhale, give whatever they might need right now—peace, patience, love, or light.

7. You can practice this anytime. During deep stress or uncertainty, I encourage you to quietly do this exercise for a few minutes once every hour to support yourself and keep your mind and heart clear and loving through a difficult situation.

CHAPTER TEN

Planting the Seeds for Happy Partnerships

For one human being to love another: that is perhaps the most difficult of all our tasks, the ultimate, the last test and proof, the work for which all other work is but preparation.

—RAINER MARIA RILKE[1]

WHEN MIKE AND I WERE FIRST MARRIED, IT SEEMED LIKE EVERY DECI-sion we made was a fight for control of something. I was convinced that whatever I wanted was right, and when he didn't agree with me, I felt he was standing in the way of *my* happiness. But one afternoon at lunch with my friend Andrew, I asked him why he thought his marriage of thirty years had been successful and enduring. He didn't hesitate before saying, "Because we understand the pleasure of compromise." I realized then that I'd never considered that Mike and I could cooperate and base our decisions on what is best for *us*—not for him or for me. I began to be more mindful of the choices we made together and recognize those that will create the conditions for health, peace, prosperity, and happiness—for both of us.

This is why Buddhists talk about *planting seeds*—it's a metaphor to remind you that your actions have consequences. Wise and skillful intentions, words, and deeds lead to positive and beneficial feelings and experiences. Unwise and unskillful intentions, words, and deeds lead to negative and unhappy feelings and experiences. So it's up to you to plant a garden with the right intentions and actions in order to get the outcome you want. Indeed, in Buddhism, one of the words for meditation is *bhavana*, which means "cultivate" or "foster"; you nurture and foster your best intentions with it so they take root and flourish. If you're mindful of the types of seeds that you planted and water them with attention and lovingkindness, you'll grow and reap the delightful fruits of a steady mind, an open heart, and a closer and more connected relationship.

If you take away just one lesson from this section of the book, I hope it's to remember that happy partnerships are possible. I've already mentioned that for a long time I didn't think this was true, and maybe that's how you feel about yourself. Maybe you're worried that you are limited in your capacity for love and kindness due to genetics or conditioning and that you will never be able to be a patient enough, compassionate enough, and mindful enough partner to live together gladly with your mate. But you *can* be the partner you want to be. I know it's possible because these practices and exercises are effective. As long as you're conscientious and consistent with your meditation and remember your intentions, you'll develop insight into your behaviors and habits and transform them.

Don't forget that neither you nor your partner have to be idealized beings to have a happy relationship, so you don't need to avoid or hide the difficulties and struggles you encounter in your marriage. Instead, you can create happiness *within* your imperfect, ever-changing, and unpredictable relationship. And please, don't get discouraged if you make mistakes again and again—I do too! When it happens, it doesn't mean you don't care, are lazy, or don't love your partner. It means you're human and imperfect just like all of us—and you can always recognize your errors, self-correct, and begin again . . . again.

Practice Ten: May All Partnerships Be Happy

This meditation is for everyone who'd like to create a deeper bond with their mate. Brain scientists say that repeating blessings and lovingkindness phrases help rewire old negative habits into new, more positive pathways toward connection and happiness, and this is how Buddhists plant positive seeds and cultivate their growth.

You're welcome to do this practice alone, but I encourage you to do it together with your partner. My husband and I meditate together regularly, and being together in silence as we offer our deepest wishes for well-being and love to ourselves, each other, and the world, has created a deep bond, a special intimacy, and an abiding closeness.

1. Sit down somewhere quiet where you won't be disturbed. Keep your devices out of reach and commit to not reading, checking email, or talking for the next fifteen minutes.

2. Close your eyes. Put your hand on your heart and rest your attention on your breathing. Feel the inhale and exhale from your navel to your nose.

3. If you're with your mate, notice their presence. You might hear their breath or sense them nearby.

4. Put your hand on your heart. Silently, imagine you and your partner in a moment of happiness and ease. See both of you, connected and loving with each other. Silently say to both of you, *May we be happy.* Continue to visualize the two of you together and offer the phrase repeatedly for at least five minutes.

5. Imagine another couple is with you, one that you know: your parents, good friends, or two people who are familiar to you from church or your neighborhood. Imagine they are standing in front of

you. Silently say to them, *May you be happy.* Continue repeating and giving these blessings to this other couple.

6. As you continue to visualize you and your partner with this other couple, start to include all the couples you know—those who are close to you and those who are strangers to you. Let yourself remember and think of all the couples throughout the entire world: couples who are rich, poor, middle class, old and young, married and unmarried, straight, LGBTQ, those with children and those without. Say silently to all of you: *May all couples be happy. May we be happy.* Keep imagining all of these partnerships and repeating these phrases to everyone for a few minutes.

7. When you conclude this meditation, be sure to thank yourself. If you're practicing with your partner, open your eyes, put your hands together at your heart, and offer each other a bow of appreciation.

SECTION II

HAPPY FAMILIES

CHAPTER ELEVEN

Be Kind

Be kind whenever possible. It is always possible.
—His Holiness the Dalai Lama[1]

WHEN I WAS YOUNG, I ENVIED THE FAMILIES I SAW ON TELEVISION: THE Huxtables on *The Cosby Show*, the Keatons on *Family Ties*, even the Bradys from *The Brady Bunch*. I wanted my family to be more like them—to have disagreements without screaming or hard feelings, to not criticize, complain, or ignore one another when annoyed, and to generally listen and respond with empathy and kindness to each other. But as I got older, I noticed that I didn't know *any* families that were as reasonable, self-reflective, or honest as those I saw on television or at the movies. And that's because such families don't exist. There are no ideal families. The members of every household are sometimes unreasonable, confused, and judgmental—because they're made up of imperfect human beings, just like you and me.

That's why it's important for you to know that your family doesn't have to be flawless to be happy and loving. As long as you're not abusing your kids or spouse, everyone's basic needs of shelter, food, and care are being met, you have relative stability and ordinary communication, you can create a happy (or happier) family. In fact, if you're reading this book, it's likely you have all the conditions and resources that you need to create the relationships you yearn for, ones that are close, empathic, and loving.

In *Anna Karenina,* Russian writer Leo Tolstoy famously wrote that "All happy families are alike; each unhappy family is unhappy in its own way," but this certainly isn't true, especially today. Your happy family could include people who share DNA—or not. It might be just one parent and one child. It can include grandparents, stepparents, stepsiblings, half-siblings, or foster children. It might be a family of origin or of choice. You might all live together or maybe you're co-parenting with your ex and his new spouse and all their kids and your children spend time in both households. In this book, *family* means a group of people living their lives together, and this chapter and the ones that follow in this section are for everyone who is a member of a family, especially if you're a parent or a child.

The first step to changing your family dynamics is to change your attention. Instead of directing your energy to all that's wrong and trying to fix it, you can bring happiness to yourself simply by noticing the positive qualities and resources of your life and your relationships that you already have and normally overlook. I saw firsthand how this lack of attention causes unhappiness for many people when my eighty-five-year-old mother-in-law, Cathy, took my husband and me to a suburban Costco near her home in Delaware. It was a busy Saturday afternoon, and the aisles were full of families of all types browsing an almost unimaginable amount and variety of food and goods. But despite this abundance, few of them seemed happy. Parents were tired and impatient, kids seemed bored and detached, and short-tempered spouses criticized each other while waiting in line. You've likely experienced this yourself, because I have too. So if you really want to create a happier family, start with what you already have. Notice all the good things you enjoy—simple things like apples and cheese, a comfy couch, a car. Observe the support you receive from other people. Simply open your awareness to the reality of your life and you'll see that every moment you're surrounded by blessings, goodness, and love.

If you're a parent, I encourage you to use the suggestions and exercises in this section not for self-help or self-improvement, but rather to offer yourself patience and kindness. It's not easy being a mother or father. It took me a long time to understand this because my mom was

When I'm with my family, I'm often distracted. If I'm cooking dinner or shopping, I might not listen or fully see other people, even sometimes talking over them or not noticing what they're doing. But no matter what is happening or how hectic it might be, it's always possible to pay attention to the people you love. Regularly take time to look at your spouse, kids, parents, whoever is near you, and say this blessing to them silently, "May you be happy."

immature, unreliable, selfish, and needy—and I blamed and hated her for it. But as I got older, I began to understand that the work, responsibility, pressure, and demands of parenthood, combined with her emotional limitations and struggles, were simply too hard for her. She was unable to properly parent, not because she didn't want to or didn't care, but because she didn't have many of the qualities required to do it, and she'd never been shown or taught the skills needed for it. When I finally recognized that my mom was a struggling human being just like me, it helped me feel much more compassion for both of us. And when you understand that you're a struggling human being too, it will help you to recognize the qualities you need to love yourself and your kids, as well as the tools that will help you do it.

Throughout this book, I emphasis that the most important factor in creating happy relationships is *kindness*. But you probably don't think that you can be kind all the time. If you're kind, how will you get your kids to stop leaving their dirty dishes in the sink? If you're kind, how can you tell your father to stop complaining about the cost of your tuition whenever you go to visit him? If you're kind, how will your spouse know that you can no longer tolerate spending every weekend alone while they go out with their friends? Despite what you might believe, I assure you it is possible to get your needs met *and* be kind when you request it. You can do this if you act when you're mindful, when your behavior isn't a result of anger or resentment, and when you speak with honesty, clarity, and directness. Behaving with unkindness, like yelling at your son or criticizing your sister, only results in distress and hurt feelings and won't give you what you truly want: consideration and understanding.

Also remember that being kind doesn't always have to be "nice." You might choose to stop lending money to your brother if he didn't pay back the last loan, but you can do it without meanness. Your words don't always have to be pleasant, and you don't need to hide your anger or disappointment, either. In fact, I encourage you to share your emotions in a nonaggressive way so your family knows how you're really feeling. Phrase it in ways like this: "I'm angry at what you did, and I want you to know how it affected me" or "I'm so sad that you forgot my birthday." If you speak directly and honestly, you're more likely to repair a rupture, because you provide the listener with an opportunity to empathize and validate your experience. You'll also feel better about yourself if you're kind. I usually feel guilty, ashamed, or mad at myself when I do or say something harsh, but when I speak mindfully and act carefully—even when I'm hurt, angry, or dissatisfied—I tend to feel steady and empowered, and you will too.

Although I've worked hard to develop patient and loving behavior and be a skillful communicator, sometimes I still say or do something sharp, overly critical, or even hostile to someone I care about. You will too; it's normal—we're all human and imperfect beings, and change takes time. Just remember, all relationships will have rifts, misunderstandings, and estrangements, even the happiest, and when you act badly, it's always possible to repair it. Acknowledge your unkindness, apologize for what you said, let it go, and start over. You don't have to ruminate over it, berate yourself, or feel guilty, but do make a commitment to pause before you speak or act in the future, especially when you're angry or upset.

Finally, you might feel like you don't have the time or energy to change your habits, or that your family is so dysfunctional it won't matter anyway—but if you're reading this book, please hear this: I *know* you can create happier relationships. That's because all the practices here, and all the Buddhist teachings from which they're derived, simply ask you to recognize and use qualities you already have: kindness, love, patience, compassion, joy, attention, and care. When you connect with all these beautiful assets, even if no one else in your family changes, your relationships will change because you will.

Given my troubled history with my own family, I had some doubts about my qualifications for writing this book. But when I told my mother-in-law what it was about, she said cheerfully, "You'll do a great job. You and I certainly have a happy relationship." That's when I realized I don't need any special credentials to share my knowledge and experience, because everyone who loves and is loved is a relationship expert, and that includes you. You have the experience, goodness, love, and most important, the sincere intention to connect with your dearest people, share their joys and sorrows, and reveal your beautiful, vulnerable, and loving self to them and the world. You have the ability to develop the confidence you need to make strong and lasting bonds, heal old wounds, and trust in your capacity for kindness, love, and connection with the people who matter most to you—your family.

Although some people might be violent and cause harm by physically injuring others, verbally abusing them, or destroying property, for most of us, the harm we cause will come from our careless, unkind, angry, or deceitful speech. You've undoubtedly experienced the power of words to damage family relationships, destroy trust, and create rifts, and that's why the Eightfold Path's way of Wise Speech is such an important tool for establishing harmony and creating a foundation of goodwill in your family. When you communicate skillfully—with kindness and care—you're letting your family know you love and respect them, even if you're saying no or delivering difficult information. Remember, Wise Speech includes what you say, the emails you send, the texts you write, and all the comments that you make on social media, too. Here are a few guidelines:

- Be Honest. Make sure your words and communications are true and not meant to misled or deceive.
- Don't malign or slander. Be sure to talk about others without disparagement or exaggeration.

- Don't be abusive. Refrain from cruel or malicious communications, words, or texts that are meant to hurt or harm someone. This includes what you say to and about yourself.

- Enjoy silence. Don't speak unless your words are useful and necessary. You don't need to fill up space and waste your time on meaningless chatter that has no use or value.

Practice Eleven: Receive What You Have

Many families don't take the time to pay attention to what they already have—each other, a place to live, food, education—and wonder why they feel dissatisfied or bored. I hope you'll do the following practice when you or your kids are feeling disinterested or comparing yourself to other people. It will help you reconnect to your resources, feel glad for your life and your loved ones, and stop worrying so much.

Find a quiet spot, sit still, and turn off your devices. Don't talk. Put your hand on your belly and count ten full breaths. Then say this silently three times:

I receive gratefully the safety and well-being I have been given.

I receive gratefully the blessings of kindness I have been given.

I receive gratefully the measure of health I have been given.

I receive gratefully the family I have been given.

If you have young children or you don't have much time, you can recite this sweet and simple old prayer that my neighbor Alice recently shared with me, instead. It expresses the same sentiment:

Thank you for the world so sweet.

Thank you for the food we eat.

Thank you for the birds that sing.

We give thanks for everything.

Chapter Twelve

Creating Boundaries

There can be a compassionate way of saying no. Saying no can actually be a generous gesture in the sense of not continuing with an unworkable relationship or situation.

—Laura Bridgman[1]

After not speaking to each other for almost five years, Danielle's mother contacted her right before Christmas. She called from the hospital after another health crisis—she was weak, tired, and emaciated. She lived in St. Louis in a house she'd inherited, and she wanted to go back there, but the doctors insisted she spend time at a rehabilitation facility. She asked Danielle, who lived on the West Coast, to visit her and said she needed help.

Just hearing her voice made Danielle irritable and anxious. Her mother was an unpredictable woman who, when younger, married and divorced several times, moved every few years, and had never held a job for very long. In childhood, Danielle and her younger brother Ben could never rely on their mom, and changing schools so often combined with financial instability made them afraid and insecure. The last thing Danielle wanted was to see her mother, but Ben lived overseas now, and her mother genuinely needed help. Danielle was flooded with fear and worry and resentment, and she wondered what she should do.

You're not alone if you have family members—parents, siblings, children—who have interpersonal difficulties and/or can't take care of themselves properly. Nearly all of us do, and we worry and fear for them, wish for them to create a stable life, and hope they will become responsible. Such people will often need and ask for your help, and chances are you've assisted them many times before. But you might be wondering if it's time to break this cycle, which may be upsetting you and doesn't seem to help them much. If so, you might consider creating healthy boundaries: emotional and physical limits to protect your well-being and peace of mind.

Dennis knew he should do this with his twenty-six-year-old son Kahlil, who struggled with depression. Kahlil didn't want to stay in treatment with his therapist, regularly take antidepressants, exercise, or stop smoking weed. He would seem steady for a month or two, then crash and hardly get out of bed. Dennis called his son often, gave him lots of advice and encouragement, and helped him financially, but the psychologist Dennis consulted suggested that he set boundaries—back off and leave Kahlil to experience some of the consequences of his actions, instead of paying for car repairs when Kahlil didn't have enough money to fix his car's broken side mirror, or calling to make or cancel medical appointments for him. The therapist thought this would help Kahlil learn from his mistakes. And Dennis's friends told him the same thing—that Kahlil was too dependent and Dennis too indulgent. But Dennis thought they wanted him to abandon Kahlil, and he couldn't do that.

> If you're struggling to deal with a relative who has mental health problems, it's useful to remember you're not alone and that there are tools and resources that can help you and them. Contact a therapist or counselor or join a support group. You can find many resources at the National Alliance for Mental Illness (NAMI). Call 1-800-950-NAMI (6264), text "HelpLine" to 62640, or email helpline@nami.org.

Many people I meet worry that they're not good or compassionate if they refuse a request for help, or don't volunteer to fix another person's problems, especially if it's someone they love. You might think this too—that saying no or setting boundaries is uncaring and that being compassionate means you'll let people walk all over you and allow their destructive behavior to continue without trying to stop it or acknowledge how it affects you. But this isn't compassion at all. Compassion includes using your wisdom to know what the most beneficial action is—for yourself and others. It's the opposite of indifference; you don't stop caring but you do recognize you can't control another person's choices no matter how hard you try.

Dennis finally realized that he was desperate to prevent Kahlil from suffering, but how he was doing it wasn't working. He knew he could never turn his back on his son, but it would help them both if Dennis stopped trying to interfere and fix Kahlil's problems. So he decided to stop, wait, and allow his son to ask for help before trying to intervene. At first it was hard for him to hear Kahlil complain about his difficulties and watch him flounder without telling him what to do or offering solutions. But Dennis began to notice a sense of relief for himself—that he could be a loving and compassionate dad while still setting limits. And he was surprised that his son felt more respected and trusted.

Danielle came to a similar conclusion. For several days after she spoke with her mom, she was anxious and depressed, resentful, and could hardly sleep because she hated her mother's neediness and her failure to care for herself or her kids. But soon after, Danielle lit a candle and said a prayer for herself and her mom. She acknowledged how upset she was and how she still wished she could save her mother and create a loving relationship. But she also realized that it wasn't up to her—her mom was going to do what she wanted, not what Danielle wanted *for* her. Danielle decided the most compassionate thing she could do was to say, "I love you, and no." She called her mom and told her she wouldn't visit, but that she cared about her and wanted to stay in touch. She was glad they were no longer estranged, that they could connect without shame or resentment, and she felt better able to accept her mother's love, however limited and flawed it might be.

Shantideva was a Buddhist monk who lived in India during the eighth century and wrote *A Guide to the Bodhisattva's Way of Life*. His text is beloved by many Buddhists today, mainly for the simplicity of his practices and his informal and personal approach to practice. Perhaps his most famous teaching—which is often quoted—is from the chapter on mindfulness:

> *Where would there be leather enough to cover the entire world? With just the leather of my sandals, it is as if the whole world were covered. Likewise, I am unable to restrain outer circumstances, but I can control my own mind. What need is there to control anything else?*[2]

I hope you'll remember this the next time you're trying to change someone so you can be content, calm, or happy. Just as wearing shoes is wiser than trying to cover the entire earth with leather to protect your feet, so is taking care of your own emotions more useful and effective than expecting other people to change.

Practice Twelve: Cultivating Compassion

Sometimes I feel so pressured to do something to fix or change a family member who is having difficulty, and if you know someone like this, you probably do too. Maybe you struggle with guilt and worry or can't let go of the idea that you need to intervene in some way. That's a signal to remember that what other people do is not up to you. This practice will help you use your wisdom and good sense to stop trying to control what you can't control and to develop compassion for both yourself and this person. Try it the next time you're feeling stressed out; after you're done, take a moment to really understand what action—if any—will truly help the situation. Remember, sometimes doing nothing is the kindest action you can take.

1. Lie down on the floor or your bed. Close your eyes and place a hand on your belly. Count five full inhales and exhales while feeling the rise and fall of your chest and abdomen.

2. Silently say to yourself, *May I recognize all the love and support in my life. May I be at peace.* Continue repeating this—like you're giving yourself a gift—for five minutes.

3. Next, think of the person you know who is struggling and who you feel obligated to fix or help, and offer the same blessing, saying silently to them, *May you recognize all the love and support in your life. May you be at peace.*

4. After a minute or two, say this phrase silently to the same person, *May I be at peace with who you are.* Repeat this for five minutes. If you get distracted or lose track of the phrases, you can start again.

5. Before you conclude the meditation, be sure to thank yourself and remember you can do this again anytime you feel frustrated, scared, or worried about anyone.

Chapter Thirteen

Navigating Anger

We have the capacity to make this world heaven, beginning with how we interact in the world. This is called divinely living—to carry love and friendliness in our hearts rather than ill will. Just as we can make hell on earth, lovingkindness practice can make heaven on earth.
—Bhante Henepola Gunaratana[1]

When Tony's daughter Lia showed up late for her shift at the pizza parlor for the third week in a row, Tony was enraged. Before the door had even closed behind her, he shouted from behind the takeout counter, saying she was irresponsible, didn't care about her family, and was taking advantage of him. Lia said nothing, but she was hurt. She went to the back, changed into her uniform, and started prepping pizza boxes for the night—but not before she texted her mother, who assured her they would work it out at home together later.

I know you've experienced something similar to this, because all families have disagreements, conflicts, and anger. It's impossible to be a parent or a child—or a human!—without arguing or getting mad at each other sometimes. But your anger doesn't have to destroy your caring connection and loving presence. You can get mad at someone, hold them accountable for their behavior, and communicate clearly and kindly, without hostility or rage. If you bring mindfulness and compassion to your feelings, you'll be able to remember that your loved one is not your enemy—they care about you, they didn't intend to cause you pain, and they want you to be happy, and you feel the same for them.

You probably already know this but I'm going to remind you anyway. When you're angry, stop! Don't do or say anything at all. Sit down and breathe, go for a walk, or have a quiet cup of tea. Wait until you calm down before engaging with any other person.

So often, damaging and reckless anger is fueled by underlying confused and hurt feelings. When my cousin heatedly disagreed with me recently about the best candidate for city council, raised his voice and talked over me, I was surprised at how quickly my irritation arose. I yelled that he was wrong, and when he saw how upset I was, he assured me that he respected my views and didn't mean to hurt me. I sat down in the kitchen and noticed my heart was racing, but I realized it wasn't because we support different politicians. It was because I thought he was dismissing my opinions as meaningless, and it wounded me.

This is the same thing that happened to Tony. He didn't want to talk to his daughter about her lateness because he thought she didn't like him and disdained their family business and it pained him. After his outburst, he was disappointed and ashamed of himself but also convinced he was not in the wrong, so there was no reason for him to apologize. But his brother, a therapist, helped Tony see that although he felt taken advantage of and ignored, his family cared about him and respected and appreciated his work. As a result, Tony sat down with his daughter and wife at dinner and explained that Lia's lateness made him feel devalued and as though he didn't matter, and as soon as he said it, he felt relieved—and his wife and daughter did too. Without his anger, they could connect and empathize with him, and when Lia reassured him that he mattered to her and apologized for her behavior and for hurting him, he was deeply touched. Tony held her hand and told Lia and his wife that he would do his best to communicate more and take better care of his feelings to prevent outbursts in the future.

I think you'll agree that it's clear that unrestrained anger is the greatest threat to our peace of mind, our relationships, and even to society and our environment. It's what drives destructive and hateful behavior, and that's why the Buddhist tradition has more teachings on this topic than any other. The Buddha explains that there are two types of anger: constructive and destructive. Constructive anger arises when you notice that you or someone else has been harmed, and this leads you to want to rectify or alleviate the cause through thoughtful and skillful action. Destructive anger also arises when you notice that you or someone else has been harmed, but instead of leading to sensible ways to resolve it, it leads to violent, unkind, or even cruel words and actions. While constructive anger is driven by wisdom, destructive anger is driven by malice and hostility. That's why destructive anger is included in the Three Poisons (the other two are greed and delusion). The Three Poisons are mind-states that cause pain and confusion and result in stupid and harmful words and actions. The Buddhist teachings insist that you take responsibility when the poisons arise in your minds and stop them from escalating so you don't suffer, cause injury, or sow division in your family.

Taryn only learned this after she nearly ruined her relationship with her oldest son. For many years, she was convinced that Fernando was disrespectful, and she demanded that he listen to her opinions and take her advice. When he didn't, she was hurt, and destructive anger arose in her heart. When he left for college, he rarely called her and she couldn't understand why. But when she finally learned through her husband that Fernando believed *she* didn't like *him* because she was constantly criticizing and belittling him, she recognized that she was hurting her son. She reached out to a church counselor who helped her identify her anger—without blame or shame. She learned to bring patience to herself, pay attention to her body and thoughts, and understand her unrealistic expectations so she could release them. Finally, she was able to reconnect with her loving presence and enjoy and appreciate her son and their relationship.

Even after reading this, you still might feel that healthy and happy families simply *shouldn't* have serious conflict or destructive anger. You might think that by definition *happy* means freedom from misunderstandings, hurt feelings, and mean words. You might feel embarrassed or even hide these difficulties from people outside of your family. I've felt this way about many things in the past, and that's why the most valuable teaching I've learned from Buddhism is that *nothing can be remedied until it's acknowledged, validated, and understood.* That's why confronting your struggles as a family—as difficult as it can be—is also deeply rewarding, and *happy.* The more you become mindful and insightful about your thoughts, feelings, and motivations, the better able you are to prevent ruptures and ensure your loved ones truly care about each other even when they're upset. You'll be able to regard challenges not as a negative reflection of you or anyone, but rather as a positive opportunity to learn and improve your communication and connection and love for each other.

"Don't take what they're giving" is an instruction from an old Buddhist story that I think about whenever a family member is angry, enraged, or frustrated. It's a reminder to me to *not* allow their behavior to sow destructive anger in my mind—which is hard to do sometimes. It's explained in an old story about how the Buddha responded to an annoying stranger. One version goes like this:

Once the Buddha was visiting a town where a man named Akkosaka lived. Akkosaka didn't like the Buddha because his nephew was one of the Buddha's students, and he and his family felt that his nephew should pursue a different path in life. So when he saw the Buddha walking on the Main Street in his village, Akkosaka heckled him from across the road. He shouted, "You're a fake! You're just in it for the money! You're a bad influence!" The Buddha stopped and calmly walked over to Akkosaka and incongruously asked him if he ever had guests to his home for dinner. Akkosaka, confused, said yes. Then the Buddha said, "If your guests don't take the food and drinks you serve them, then who do the food and drinks belong to?" Akkosaka, even more bewildered, replied, "Well, I guess they still belong to me." The Buddha nodded, smiled, and said kindly, "Exactly. And in just the same way, you offered me your anger, but I won't take what you're giving me. Your anger remains with you." He politely bowed to Akkosaka and continued on his way.

Practice Thirteen: Patience

I suggest you do the following practice as soon as you realize you're feeling angry. If you wait and your anger grows, it will be harder to calm your
body and mind—but not impossible! Just pay attention to your breathing, hands, and stomach; they often indicate you're feeling distressed
even before you notice it in your thoughts. If your anger is powerful and
destructive, then be sure to stop talking and exhale longer than your
inhale for several minutes. It will calm your nervous system enough to
do this exercise.

1. Sit down and put your hand on your heart. You don't have to do
   anything else, just sit there and don't get up.

2. After a few minutes, pay attention to your anger. Where do you
   sense it in your body? Are your fists clenched or is your stomach
   upset? Where do you feel it in your mind? Are you thinking no one
   cares or that they're wrong or it's all their fault? Keep breathing and
   allowing your anger to be here. Don't let yourself get caught in a
   story about anything.

3. In five minutes, you can inhale deeply and put (or keep) your hand
   on your heart. Then say to yourself silently, *May I be patient with
   myself. May I be free.* Repeat this to yourself for a few minutes.

4. Then think of the person you're angry with. Imagine they're here
   with you. Say to them, *May I be patient with you. May you be free.*
   Repeat this silently for several minutes.

5. Finally, recognizing that all families and people have disagreements
   and anger, silently say these phrases to everyone, *May we be patient
   with ourselves and each other. May we be free.*

6. Be sure to thank yourself before concluding this meditation. And
   know that you can repeat it as often as needed.

CHAPTER FOURTEEN

Dealing with Addiction

Not every story has a happy ending, but the discoveries of science, the teachings of the heart, and the revelations of the soul all assure us that no human being is ever beyond redemption. The possibility of renewal exists so long as life exists. How to support that possibility in others and in ourselves is the ultimate question.

—GABOR MATÉ[1]

WHEN I WAS A CHILD, ALL THE ADULTS AROUND ME DRANK. MY PARents often had a glass of wine or beer with dinner after work, and on the weekends they, their families, and their friends all enjoyed drinking together at parties, barbecues, and bars. It seemed harmless and fun. But as I grew older, I could see that my mom wasn't like the other adults. She didn't just have one or two drinks—she kept drinking until my dad told her to stop or she was so tired she fell asleep on the couch. She hid empty bottles so he couldn't see what she was doing, but after they divorced, she didn't hide it anymore. When I was twenty years old, living in an apartment with a friend and attending college, I went to visit her at home on a Sunday afternoon. She was sitting at the kitchen table talking to someone on the phone and when I walked in the room, my mom asked if I wanted to talk to Aunt Milly and handed me the phone before I could even respond. My aunt said, "Your mom's drunk again," and I didn't know what to say. It was the first time anyone had acknowledged her drinking habit to me. I felt surprised and embarrassed, yet relieved. That evening at my best friend Lori's house, I said for the first time in my life, "I think my mother is an alcoholic."

There are many definitions of what constitutes an addiction, but here I'm using it to mean a compulsive behavior that you can't control and that you prioritize over nearly everything else in your life, including your relationships. Many people view it as a vice or a moral failing, which is why there is a lot of shame and embarrassment about it, and also why people don't often talk about it. But there are very few people I encounter who aren't affected in some way by addiction. Maybe you're dependent on alcohol or cannabis use. Maybe someone in your family wrestles with prescription opioids or is in recovery for a sex addiction. Whoever it is that's struggling, one thing is certain—their problem affects everyone in your family, and their behavior is causing deep suffering, for them and for everyone who loves them.

In Buddhism, we understand the cause of addiction as a mind-state that everyone experiences, called *tanha*. The literal translation of this word is "thirst," and it means craving, desire, or longing. Everyone is familiar with the suffering caused by *tanha*—it's the clinging feeling you get when you want so much for something wonderful to happen, and it's the heart-breaking desperation you have when you don't want something terrible to happen. What we call addiction is simply an extreme form of *tanha*—an obsessive and all-encompassing need to feel happy, at ease, and free from pain and struggle. *Tanha* is related to our desire to feel good and not feel bad, and this is the reason people begin using drugs: cocaine, sex, vodka. At first it works—drugs help to cope and manage stress and pain. But sadly, the more we use them, the less effective they become, and we need more and more to reach a baseline satisfaction. Soon a simple craving for happiness becomes a compulsion that leads us into deeper unhappiness.

My mom's alcoholism prevented her from truly connecting with me, and for a long time, I was angry at her because I believed she should just stop drinking. I couldn't understand why she continued because it was obviously detrimental to her life, her health, and her relationships. Her house was a mess, she had emphysema from smoking, and the only people she spent time with were other drinkers like her. You might be wondering the same thing I did: why can't you easily quit watching internet porn or why doesn't your sister just stop smoking pot every night? But now I understand that it's because what began as a simple way to manage pain, anxiety, or trauma has now become the only coping mechanism available to deal with difficulties, stress, and emotional pain.

That's what happened to Ray. During the 2020 pandemic, he and his wife, Angela, isolated together for over a year with their one-year-old baby in a small bungalow. Most nights they were both relieved after their son went to sleep, and Angela happily read a book in bed alone, while Ray played online poker on the computer in the basement. He missed his friends and even missed going to the office, which was ironic because he'd complained so often about the long commute. His wife was mostly involved with the baby, and he felt excluded by their bond. He became lonely, felt abandoned, and started exploring internet porn. He'd watched it for pleasure occasionally in the past, and even sometimes watched it with Angela, who enjoyed it too. But this time it was different. Over the next year, he increasingly spent time alone in his basement, watching videos of people having sex, and masturbating for hours.

He hid what he was doing from Angela, but he knew she sensed there was a problem. She noticed that he was impatient and disinterested in spending time with his family, but she didn't know why. It wasn't until Angela saw notifications on his phone from an OnlyFans account and confronted him that he realized he had a problem. When he tried to quit, he couldn't—because anytime he experienced stress, he felt compelled to watch a sex video and masturbate. It helped . . . but not for long. Ray finally found a therapist who specialized in sex addiction and he came to understand his triggers and redevelop healthy coping skills like meditation, journaling, and exercise. Ray and Angela went to couples counseling and were able to restore their connection and recommit to each other and their son.

If you or someone you love has an addiction, there are resources available to help you recover, and many of these are free of charge. If one type of treatment or therapy doesn't work, keep trying. Whatever happens, don't give up because the more often someone tries to end an addiction—no matter how many times they fail—the more likely they are to successfully recover and heal from it.

Poignantly, not everyone will recover from an addiction, and for the people who love them this is heartbreaking and sad. My mom couldn't stop drinking, even during the last year of her life when she was very sick and doctors explained that consuming alcohol was worsening her condition. I (and others who loved her and worried for her) threatened and begged her to stop, until one day after yelling at her for being drunk again, I realized I couldn't keep doing it. I thought about equanimity—the fourth type of love in the Four Immeasurables. This Buddhist quality of profound wisdom recognizes we're not in charge of everything and we can't control other people's actions. I realized I could stop attempting to manage her alcohol consumption and trying to get her to listen to her doctors' advice—and I could still love her. The traditional equanimity contemplation is *Regardless of my wishes for you, your happiness is not in my hands. May you be at peace.* I repeated this phrase for my mom many times until she died a few months later. If you're struggling to accept that someone in your family has an addiction, I hope you'll consider doing this practice too. It really helped me feel less responsible, more open, and freer to love—myself and my mom too.

Buddhism recognizes that intoxicants destroy our ability to see clearly and impair our capacity to appropriately love and care for ourselves and each other. This is why Buddhist monastics and students traditionally take a vow to abstain from taking drugs or alcohol—not because it's a moral failing or a sin, but because when we're drunk, stoned, or high, it's easy to become greedy, demanding, judgmental, or self-centered.

The Buddha described intoxicants as any substance that "clouds the mind," and in his time that meant alcohol and drugs like soma, bhang, or datura, all with psychotropic properties. But in modern life there are many things that can cloud our mind, and that's why today this vow also includes a commitment to stop mindlessly watching television, getting lost in social media, or participating in violent video games or destructive movies. Anything that creates delusions and sweeps us away from reality or leads us to harmful behavior is an intoxicant that we should avoid.

Practice Fourteen: Equanimity

When someone you love is struggling, it's understandable that you want to help them in any way you can. This is especially true when you can see that they are causing themselves harm, especially with drugs, alcohol, or another compulsive behavior. You might try to manage their addiction by attempting to keep them away from certain situations or by monitoring where they go and what they do, to prevent them from making bad decisions. But ultimately, it's not in your power to change another person's behavior, no matter how much you love them.

Equanimity, the fourth type of love from the Four Immeasurables, is the wisdom that allows us to stop trying to control anyone else. Although it's very painful to watch someone make bad mistakes again and again, equanimity gives us the strength and courage to let go of our demands that they act differently. Equanimity enables us to keep our hearts open, even as we accept that someone we love will continue to suffer because of their own confused actions or refusal to ask for help. The following meditation is both heartbreaking and enlightening. It will ground you and give you strength. I hope you'll practice it often.

1. Find a quiet and comfortable place where you won't be disturbed. You can lie down, sit, or walk—whatever feels most gentle and easy for you. Put your hand on your belly and notice your breath. Keep breathing.

2. Offer yourself lovingkindness meditation. Imaging you're looking at yourself in the mirror, with tenderness. Place one hand on your heart and another on your belly. Repeat these phrases to yourself, *May I be gentle with myself. May I be peaceful and at ease.* If you get lost, take a breath and begin again.

3. Now imagine the person that you love who has an addictive behavior. Feel their presence with you as you say this phrase

silently: *Regardless of my wishes for you, your happiness is not in my hands.* Remember, you can always go back to step 1 and start again.

4. You can also try these other, similar phrases. Use whichever feels most natural to you, or create your own: *You're responsible for the suffering or happiness created by your own actions. May you find a true source of happiness. May you find peace exactly where you are.*

5. After a few minutes or whenever you're ready, stop saying the phrases and quietly feel the rise of your belly as you breathe. Take a minute to offer lovingkindness to all of us struggling and confused humans by saying silently: *May we—may everyone—be gentle with ourselves. May we all be at peace.* Then be sure to appreciate your wisdom and good heart.

6. Before you conclude this meditation, take time to let yourself be quiet and still. You can offer yourself comfort and put your hand on your heart or gently stroke your face before you resume your regular activities.

Chapter Fifteen

Loving Difficult Family Members

When you recognize that pain and response to pain is a universal thing, it helps explain so many things about others, just as it explains so much about yourself. It teaches you forbearance. It teaches you a moderation in your responses to other people's behavior. It teaches you a sort of understanding. It essentially tells you what everybody needs. You know what everybody needs? You want to put it in a single word? Everybody needs to be understood. And out of that comes every form of love.

—Dr. Sherwin Nuland[1]

My neighbor Shekar has an extraordinarily difficult ex-wife. While they were married, she yelled at him if he didn't like the same things she did, including wearing matching colors and eating the same foods. When he traveled for business, she demanded he call her every morning and evening, and when he did, she criticized him for being away. Although they divorced a decade ago, they co-parent two children, and any interaction with her inevitably means blame, disapproval, or shame. When I saw him for coffee recently, he was upset and told me that she had become irrationally angry when she found out the cost of the new clothes dryer he and his now-wife purchased for their house. She told their daughter that he was selfish for spending so much money on his new family and not on his "first" family. Exasperated and angry, Shekar said, "Kim, can you believe she said that?" I said, "Yes, I can believe she did that! I'd be surprised if she didn't! That's who she is!" and we both laughed.

Wanting someone in their family to be anyone other than who they are may be the single most common struggle people tell me about, and every family has at least one difficult person like this: the father who turns his children's problems into something about him, the adulterous cousin who's been married three times, the brother who doesn't stop talking about himself, and the sullen niece who refuses to make eye contact. If you know someone who behaves consistently and predictably badly, but you're surprised each time they do so, then they're no longer the problem—you are. You're wanting them to be different than they are. As the Buddhist teacher Larry Rosenberg likes to say, "You're wishing a chicken to be a duck."

If you finally decide to accept someone as who they are, it means you don't have to continue to suffer by trying to get them to give you something they can't, or be disappointed over and over when they don't do as you'd like or wish. It doesn't mean you agree with them or approve of their bad behavior, but rather that you're using your wisdom to see them clearly so you can interact with them *as they are, not as you wish they would be*. In Buddhism, this is called "discernment"—the ability to see reality just as it is, without it being obscured by your wishes, desires, or fantasies.

This was hard for John. His mother, Florence, lived a few blocks from him, his wife Nisha, and their two kids, Will and Tabby. Will and Tabby were often visiting their grandma's house, playing with her old cats and helping with her vegetable garden. But Florence had always been insensitive when she felt stressed or irritated, so John wasn't surprised when one humid Sunday afternoon, Tabby came home and sat on the couch and tearfully said, "Grandma told me to shut up." John replied, "She's in a bad mood because of the heat. You shouldn't go over there when the weather is like—" but before he could finish, Nisha interrupted him. She looked at her husband and her daughter and said firmly, "It's not Tabby's fault when someone is unkind to her. Grandma said something mean and that hurts. Period."

John realized he'd been making excuses for his mother his entire life because he wanted to think of her as a loving, kind, and wonderful parent. And she was . . . sometimes. Nisha helped him see how his wishes obscured the truth, and as he accepted how difficult she could be, he saw that he could protect his kids from her impatience and sharp words.

> Just because someone is a family member, it doesn't mean they're allowed to harm you or anyone else. If they say or do something mean, unkind, or hurtful, don't let it continue. Tell them their behavior is painful and end the encounter. If appropriate, leave. If you're on the phone, end the call.

Loving your frustrating family members doesn't mean that you must like them, give in to their demands, or even spend time with them. It simply means you don't need to keep wishing they were different or hating them for who they are. With good reason, Shekar will likely never like his ex-wife. But with patience and lovingkindness, he no longer tries to justify her demands, revile her, wish she would be less troublesome, or defend himself when she's upset with him. This might not sound easy to do—and it does take determination—but I know it's possible. My student Ivy is a great example. She's struggled for nearly a decade with intense feelings of hatred for her brother's girlfriend, Olivia. Olivia is an unpredictable person who has created many divisions in Ivy's family through gossip and lies and has insulted and verbally attacked Ivy many times. Although Ivy did her best to keep her distance from Olivia, and refrained from responding unkindly, in Ivy's heart she felt angry and hostile. When I suggested she offer lovingkindness to Olivia, to soothe her *own* heart, Ivy insisted she could never like Oliva enough to wish her well. That's when I explained that lovingkindness doesn't have to be a warm and fuzzy feeling of happiness and delight about someone you don't like. Sometimes it's simply enough for hatred to be transformed into nonhatred for you to feel better.

After about a year of practicing lovingkindness meditation, Ivy told me that she doesn't detest or loathe Olivia anymore. She still doesn't like her, but she no longer wishes her harm or finds her presence unbearable.

Ivy simply feels a sense of patience, forbearance, and tolerance—for herself and for Ivy—and compassion for her brother who's often torn between his girlfriend and the rest of his family.

It isn't easy but you can do this too. Instead of letting yourself get frustrated, angry, or confused, wondering, "Why won't he just stop complaining?" or "She needs to see a therapist, can't she see that?," try the approach Ivy used. Remember this person wants to be happy, to have a sense of peace and ease, to feel free from strife and struggle—just like you do. You can silently wish them contentment, or imagine they're relaxing in a pleasant and peaceful place. Remember, when you give lovingkindness to this person, it doesn't mean you agree with their behavior or want them to continue it. It only means that giving up *your* disgust, animosity, and aversion will make *you* feel better.

A common Buddhist saying is that "Everyone is your teacher," including those you don't like. A famous example of this is the story told about Atisha, the revered Buddhist master who lived in ancient India. When he traveled to Tibet, he was accompanied by a tea boy who was irritating, incompetent, and generally unpleasant. When asked by his students why he continued to employ such a wearisome person, Atisha surprised them when he responded, "He's my greatest teacher." You can take the same attitude toward your difficult family members and friends. Rather than regard them as an obstacle to be overcome or a nuisance to be avoided, you can remember who they really are—your greatest teachers, showing you your greatest challenges.

Practice Fifteen: Love Meditation

I've spent a lot of time trying to change other people. Getting my father to vote for a different candidate, persuading my dear friend to not be so sad about her breakup with a jerk, even trying to get strangers to agree with our neighborhood Open Street initiative instead of protesting it. Sometimes it works, but mostly, trying to change someone else's mind is an exercise in futility and frustration—for me and for them.

That's because how others view the world isn't in your control. You can do your best, but you can't make them see things your way, even if they're totally wrong or dangerous. If you keep pushing, all that will result is more frustration and aggravation—for you and for them. The next time you're in this situation, I encourage you to use this exercise. And if you know you're going to see someone difficult in the future, you can do this practice in advance as a way to help make your next encounter less upsetting.

1. The first step is just to notice that you're bothered, displeased, or exasperated with someone. If so, stop talking.

2. Find a quiet spot, get still, and shut off your devices. Sit quietly and take a few deep inhales and exhales for several minutes.

3. Now, put your hand on your heart and feel whatever feelings and sensations are here. Silently say to yourself, *May I accept this moment as it is. May I be at peace.* Repeat for a few minutes.

4. Next, connect with the person who has upset you. Imagine they're sitting here with you, or visualize them as a child. Say to them silently, *May I accept you as you are. May you be at peace.* As you repeat these sentences, offer them as though they are gifts.

5. After at least five minutes, you can share these lovingkindness phrases with everyone. Say silently, *May everyone accept each other as we are. May everyone be at peace.*

CHAPTER SIXTEEN

No Good and No Bad Parents

People talk about the American dream, in which your kids have a bet-ter life than you do. And we always think about it materialistically. But I think about it psychologically and spiritually—changing the legacy of how you were raised and handing your kids a new default that is kinder and more humane and wiser.

—TERRENCE REAL[1]

DEENA WAS DETERMINED TO BE A GOOD MOM. DEENA'S FATHER HAD left her family when she was two years old, and her mother, Jean, strug-gled to raise Deena and her brother, Jimmy, by herself, with little support and only a nursing aide's salary. She worked the swing shift, so Deena and Jimmy learned to cook and clean when they were quite young, and Deena often wished her mom could read to her before bed and take them out to Panera and the Olive Garden like her friends' parents did. So when Deena's daughter Michelle was born, Deena was determined to not be anything like her mother. Instead of paying half-hearted attention to Michelle's schooling, she volunteered for every event and field trip. Instead of making Michelle do chores, Deena did all the cooking, laun-dry, and cleaning. She prided herself on being a much better mother than Jean. And in many ways, she was. But just because she wasn't like her own mother didn't mean she was perfect. So she was surprised when Michelle was twelve and made a face after hearing that Deena would be going to the movies with her and her friends instead of just dropping them off at the theater like the other parents did. Michelle quipped, "Don't you have your own friends?" and Deena was deeply hurt. Wasn't she a good mom?

At first, she felt extremely guilty and wondered if despite her best efforts she had been a terrible parent. But after talking with a counselor, she understood that it wasn't about bad or good. Deena realized that by avoiding her mother's "mistakes," she'd been blind to her own and needed to reassess her approach to parenting. It was about owning her faults and learning from them. She apologized to Michelle and learned to notice when she was trying to use her daughter to ease her own feelings of loneliness and insecurity. The humility she discovered made her empathize with her mom, whom she realized shared the same struggles Deena did.

If you're a parent, I want you to stop calling yourself (and any other parent) *good* or *bad*. I want you to stop judging and comparing yourself to other people and families because it's not helping you or your children. If you're overly concerned about being good, it will make it hard for you to admit or see your mistakes and you'll keep making them, like Deena did. If you insist that you're doing it badly, you'll feel guilty and ashamed, and you'll avoid addressing mistakes. When you're able to simply see yourself as an ordinary mother or father, just like all mothers and fathers, doing your best, messing up sometimes because you're human—then you'll be better able to self-correct when needed, let go of your mistakes without self-pity or self-hatred, and begin again.

All parents have and will make countless errors—and don't forget, offer countless blessings, too. It's okay. Blunders and oversights are not a problem unless you avoid or deny them, so it's valuable to notice and learn when you've screwed up, said the wrong thing, reacted badly, or misunderstood a situation. But because parenting is such a sensitive role, it's important to approach your flaws with deep kindness and compassion for yourself. Making a mistake doesn't mean anything about you—it doesn't make you *bad*. And not making mistakes doesn't mean anything either—it doesn't make you *good*.

In the Buddhist tradition we talk about letting go, being less attached, not clinging. Most of us associate this with hanging on to things that make us happy or bring us pleasure: how to stop regretting a relationship that we wish didn't end, refusing to throw out a threadbare pair of sneakers that we love, or wishing that you could stay on your beach vacation forever. But you probably also cling to things that cause you pain and displeasure, especially your perceived shortcomings: that time when you insisted your son wear trousers to a party and everyone else wore jeans, the flash of anger in the car when your kids are talking loudly, your disappointment that your twins won't clean their rooms while you're unwilling to hold them accountable for their actions. These are the mistakes, errors, and imperfections that all parents—and people—share, but that you grasp on to as evidence that you're just not a good father or mother.

Clinging to your errors doesn't make you less likely to commit them, because it's impossible *not* to make them. It's the nature of being human that you can't know all the answers, you'll sometimes misunderstand directions and requests, and you'll often overlook or not notice something you said or did that was unskillful. Even with constant vigilance and diligence, you'll still be imperfect—and that's okay! This is why Buddhist wisdom teaches you not to get attached to your mistakes and what you think they mean about you. Instead of judging yourself, the wisest thing you can do for yourself and your kids is to just let yourself accept your faults and see them clearly. Then you can admit them and apologize or make amends for any hurt you've caused, learn to not do the same thing again, and gently let them go.

> I once asked a child psychologist what she thought made a good parent and she said, "The ability to self-correct." Please remember, all parents are wrong sometimes, misunderstand, and occasionally cause harm. But skillful and kind parents are able to acknowledge their errors, recognize the impact they have on their children, and choose to do better next time.

It might be hard to accept that some of your actions are hurting your kids, especially if, unlike Deena, you feel your parents did an excellent job and you want to emulate them. That happened to Dan. He came from a typical military family: his dad was organized, disciplined, and expected his kids would follow the rules, and they usually did, especially Dan. He was a lot like his father, and he thought that was admirable, but his wife and kids often found him rigid and inflexible, unable to know when to let go of his expectations or break a "rule" that wasn't sensible. After his ten-year-old daughter sobbed because he refused to let her go swimming on the first warm Saturday in May because she hadn't finished her homework yet, his wife angrily told him they were not in the army, and Dan realized she might be right. He began to notice how he relied on rules (that he made up!) and on his own parents' way of parenting instead of making decisions for each situation. He also realized his rigidity arose from his own anxiety and worry and remembered how fearful he'd been when he was a child because he and his siblings were so seldom allowed to be carefree or relax.

Dan realized he didn't have to keep responding like this, and the next time he and his family were hiking at the nearby state park, he noticed a woman playing fetch with a young golden retriever mix in the field by the old ranger's station. Dan got angry. He knew dogs weren't allowed off-leash in the park and he was about to say something to its owner when the dog ran up the path to greet them. As the dog dropped his ball at Dan's feet and eagerly wagged his tail and waited for Dan to play with him, he could feel his kids and wife wondering how he would respond. Dan felt his heart soften as looked into the eyes of this friendly and happy creature, and he picked up the tennis ball and threw it into the meadow. The dog sprang toward it with delight—and Dan's kids cheered and looked at their father with surprise and glee. He felt warm and happy, realizing he didn't have to parent like his dad or mom, or like anyone except himself.

Buddhism doesn't have particular rules and it's not prescriptive. The Eightfold Path suggests that each of us practice wise speech, skillful livelihood, mindfulness, and more—but unlike other religions Buddhism doesn't tell you what to do in any particular instance. Buddhism teaches us to simply let wisdom and compassion guide us in every moment, which sometimes means we act helpfully and other times refrain from doing anything at all.

There's a Zen *koan* or teaching story from the nineteenth century that is a great reminder of the importance of using your own true clarity, connection, and kindness to lead you, instead of relying on rules, commandments, or vows. It goes like this:

> *A wealthy landowner with a large country estate supported a monk for many years. He lived in a cottage on her property, and she provided him with food and his basic needs, so he could devote his time to meditation, contemplation, and Zen study. One day, a teenage girl from the village came to the monk's hut. She confessed she was madly in love with the monk and yearning for him to return her love. He moved away from her in disgust and said sternly, "I'm a monk! I don't have love affairs! You have to get out of here!" The wealthy patron saw the girl run out of the hut in tears and went to the monk to ask him what happened. After he told her, she said, "Monk! You've learned nothing in the twenty years you've been here! Pack your bags and leave!"**

*If you don't understand why the patron evicted the monk, I encourage you to sit with the story for a while. If you can't figure it out, I'll give you a hint—the reason is because he didn't follow the most important instruction in this book, explicitly mentioned in chapter 11.

Practice Sixteen: Cultivating Self-Compassion

Self-compassion is necessary for true well-being, and it includes being a good friend to yourself. As a parent, that means knowing that you'll make mistakes and have disagreements with your children and that it's okay. I encourage you to practice this meditation when you feel guilty or badly about your words or your actions, to remind yourself that you're imperfect, doing your best, and that's okay. You're still a loving and compassionate person.

1. Begin by finding a quiet place. You can sit or lie down on your bed, a couch, or the floor. Sit in the bathroom or in your car if you can't find another room in your house where you can be undisturbed. Close your eyes and put your hand on your heart. Take a few deep breaths for a few minutes.

2. Notice your emotions about your mistake or error. You might sense shame, guilt, and/or frustration with yourself. You might notice you're trying to blame someone else for what you did or said. Whatever you're experiencing is okay; just breathe into it without trying to change it or reject it or judge it.

3. Next, imagine you're looking in the mirror at yourself. See your face and feel your presence with your hand on your heart. Say to yourself, *May I allow myself to be imperfect. May I learn from my mistakes. May I be at ease.* Repeat these phrases silently for a few minutes. Notice if you get caught in a story or a memory and if you do, stop. Begin again, come back to the phrases and your connection with your warm presence.

4. Now think of your child or children. Imagine they're sitting next to you and say: *May I allow you to be imperfect. May you learn from your mistakes. May you be at ease.* Continue silently, repeating the words again and again.

5. After five minutes or so, call to mind all the parents and children that you know, including those you don't like. Imagine you're all together in a park or at the school. And say to all of you, *May we allow ourselves to be imperfect. May we learn from our mistakes. May we be at ease.*

CHAPTER SEVENTEEN

Creating a Loving Home

Cultivate the spirit of blessing. If you bless those around you this will inspire you to be attentive in every moment.

—DIPA MA[1]

GROWING UP, MY FAMILY HAD MOMENTS OF FUN AND PLEASURE, LIKE when we went to a lake house in the summer or visited my favorite aunt for Sunday dinner. But we didn't have a happy or loving home. Both of my parents were easily overwhelmed and regarded their relationships with each other and me as more of a duty and obligation than a pleasure. They were suspicious of fun or levity—in fact, my mother and her family used to say, "If you sing before breakfast, you'll cry before dinner," which more or less encapsulated their depressing view of life and relationships.

A loving home is a place where you, your kids, friends, and the members of your extended family feel comfortable, safe, and relaxed. It doesn't matter if you live in a small apartment or a six-bedroom house with a pool, or if you're a good cook or not. All that's necessary for a happy home is that when people are there, they feel accepted and loved for who they are. No one has to be successful or attractive or take care of someone else to feel valued, appreciated, and welcome—and that includes you.

Jermina didn't grow up in a happy home either. Although they were financially comfortable, her father was strict and demanding. An immigrant, he owned a thriving barbershop and believed in the value of hard work. He insisted she and her siblings consider their studies as their job, even in grammar school—"I have to work and you have to work," he told them. Jermina and her sisters never relaxed on the couch together or sat around and watched television, or hung out in the kitchen and played board games with friends. They had schoolwork and chores to take care of, and any leisure time was expected to be filled with academic clubs or volunteering. The result was that Jermina and her sisters were all excellent students, attended good colleges, and became successful professionals—but they didn't know how to enjoy themselves. Jermina was comfortable at her law firm, where her intelligence and diligence were valued, but at home, she was always tense and busy, and her kids felt it. She noticed how they and her husband tensed up and stopped laughing if she walked in a room, and she remembered feeling the same way around her dad. So she knew she had to learn to find pleasure in being at home—not just for herself, but for her family too.

> The next time you're at home, notice when you find your gaze or attention is landing on the most dissatisfying aspects of your household. When you're thinking, "That shelf is filthy," "He always leaves his glass on the table," or "Why do they have the television on all the time?" take a breath. Remember something you love about them or your life together. Then, if you still want to say or do anything, do it with patience and kindness.

So many homes feel like Jermina's—not exactly unhappy, but not happy either. A big reason for this is because many parents, maybe you too, feel they just don't have the time or energy to relax, to sit down and enjoy their family because each day is so busy: getting kids to school, going to work, doing laundry, cooking, cleaning, and more. If this is true for you, it's okay to feel overworked and exhausted—because you are. But you might be adding unnecessary stress to your already hectic life by refusing to tolerate even one dirty dish in the sink overnight or not letting anyone sleep past ten on the weekends. You might be over-looking the joy of just watching a movie with your family because you're excessively focused on performance and productivity, like good grades or athletic accomplishments. Also, if you consider your space as a place run and ruled by adults only, where your kids have no input, then of course they won't feel at ease when you're there. And if you only focus on the difficulties of running a household: the brother who always drops by at dinnertime, in-laws who insist you host the holidays, or children who don't do what you tell them to do, you'll feel dissatisfied and unhappy too. But if you can learn to welcome everyone who enters your house with goodwill, as a beloved guest and share the blessings that you have, everyone will feel much more at ease and glad, including you.

A popular misconception about Buddhism is that it is a dour and cheerless religion because of its emphasis on alleviating suffering and renouncing destructive speech and overconsumption. But the opposite is true. Buddhism encourages you to have fun, create lightness, and enjoy the positive circumstances of your life, including what you have and your relationships with others. That's because if you don't, you'll only perceive the negative and unwanted situations and overlook all the blessings you have. That's why the Buddhist practices of kindness and openness teach us to experience each moment as it is, which means we can relax, allow ourselves to enjoy our resources, and feel content with who we are. Even if your house is a mess or you're a stressed-out single parent embarrassed that you're ordering pizza for dinner for the third time this week, you can create ease and space, and a slower-paced environment, where you can appreciate yourself and the people you love. It just takes a little mindfulness practice and a willingness to hold on less tightly to what you believe needs to be done and the way you think things and people ought to be.

Brandon discovered this after weeks of planning and preparing a family party in his backyard. He wanted to celebrate and enjoy the beautiful deck they just finished building, but though the forecast predicted clear skies and warm weather, when the day came it was overcast and rainy. Instead of sitting in the sunshine on the lounge chairs, everyone sat in the living room talking and watching the baseball game. Brandon was alternately complaining about the Weather Channel's incompetence and apologizing to his family. He wouldn't sit down and couldn't relax until his partner, Tim, said, "Stop, everything is fine, stop it. Look around." He did and saw the kids playing with Legos on the kitchen table, and his mom and dad and his siblings laughing. Tim said, "You're a very lucky man." Brandon stood for a moment and let himself take it all in—the love of his family, his safe and lovely home, their health. He smiled and joined Tim on the rainy deck and helped him light the grill.

If you visit a Buddhist temple, you'll likely see people lighting candles at an altar and making offerings at a shrine. Although some of them are asking the Buddha for help, others are making prayers and blessings to develop their own heart. That's because prayer affects the mind of the person who prays. It directs your attention and focus to the many struggles in the world and connects you to them with compassion and mindfulness. It helps you recognize the preciousness of life and how lucky you are.

That's why an enjoyable and easy way to contribute to a loving home is to offer daily blessings for your family and household. The following is a prayer that I like to give in the morning or when I'm feeling dissatisfied or annoyed. I usually sit down at the kitchen table, close my eyes, and say it silently and you can too:

"I'm grateful for this safe and comfortable home. May all who live here be kind to themselves and each other."

You can practice giving blessings anytime in other ways, by making up prayers for different times of day or different tasks. The next time you're taking out the garbage or cleaning the kitchen, you can say, "I'm glad for a home to clean. May my family live together peacefully, or May all who enter our home be healthy and happy." You don't need to worry if your words will be perceived or your wishes fulfilled by a god or a higher power. It only matters that you hear, understand, and honor them.

Practice Seventeen: Cultivating Joy

If you're depleted, burned-out, or tired from the responsibilities of work and family, you'll probably find it hard to feel grateful and loving at home. You might be too tired to appreciate your material and financial resources and the people who care about you. The following meditation will help you reconnect to your love and blessings, and remember that they're always here and supporting you, even when you're discontented, exhausted, or annoyed.

1. Put your devices out of reach, get still, and stop talking.

2. Sit down in a place where you feel safe and happy. This could be your kitchen, the backyard, even the bathtub. Set a timer for ten minutes, then say to yourself, "I will stay here until the alarm rings."

3. Put one hand on your heart and the other on your belly. Take ten deep inhales and full exhales.

4. Imagine someone who has offered kindness to you is sitting next to you wherever you are. Choose someone loving—though likely not perfect—with whom you don't have conflict or ill will. They could be a family member, old friend, teacher, therapist, medical person, or spiritual mentor. This person is called your *benefactor*.

5. Visualize your benefactor looking at you. Sense their kindness and sincere affection for you as they look in your eyes. You might imagine they put their hand on your heart or gently touch your face.

6. Now imagine you hear the benefactor say to you, *May you be healthy and safe. May you be content and at ease with yourself.* Hear the benefactor repeat these phrases to you. Let yourself listen and accept and receive these blessings for several minutes.

7. Continue to imagine you and your benefactor together. And as your benefactor stops saying the phrases to you, imagine you begin saying it to your benefactor. As if you're giving them a gift, repeat these words silently, *May you be healthy and safe. May you be content and at ease with yourself.*

8. You can continue to practice this way, taking turns hearing your benefactor giving blessings to you, and saying blessings to your benefactor in return, for as long as you like and as often as you like. When you're finished, be sure to notice your surroundings, appreciate yourself for your good heart, and say thanks to this benefactor and all the many beings who've shown you kindness and encouragement.

Chapter Eighteen

Planting the Seeds for Happy Families

If you have three or four children under the age of six, your kitchen floor is not going to be spotless—unless you're the kind of parent who thinks that a shining kitchen is more important than family. And some of us have grown up in families like that. In cases like this something is backwards. A concept is not seen as merely a concept—it's seen as the Truth. "Kitchens should be clean. It's bad if kitchens are not clean." To fulfill our concepts we'll ruin families, nations, anything. All wars are based on concepts.

—Charlotte Joko Beck[1]

For over a decade, my chosen family (Lori, Denise, my niece Madeleine, and others close to us) and I vacationed annually at the beach on Fire Island off the coast of New York City in a town called Fair Harbor. Fair Harbor can only be reached by ferry and has no cars, so the house we rented always provided a few beat-up, rusty bikes to ride around the boardwalks. When Madeleine was nine years old, she rode with a friend to the lighthouse at the far end of the island. Like all the other visitors, when they arrived they left their bikes in the dunes nearby and trudged through the sand the rest of the way. But when they returned to collect the bikes for the ride home, Madeleine's was gone. It had been stolen, and she was incredulous and shocked. "Why did this happen to me?" she asked, in tears, when she returned. We assured her that it wasn't her fault, reminded her that bike theft was common on the island, and that it wasn't personal. The thief had not selected Madeleine to rob. They simply seized an opportunity to take an unattended bike.

But I later wondered why Madeleine—and all of us—notice when things go wrong and wonder why bad things happen, but generally overlook things that go right and rarely wonder why good things occur. We'd visited Fair Harbor for many years, and no one in our family—including me—ever said incredulously, "Wow, here we are in this beautiful place again! Why is this wonderful thing happening to us?"

I want you to know that wonderful things are happening to you and all our families all the time, and I hope this book helps you see it. But even after you do, you'll likely still have moments of deep sadness and loss, of disaster and illness and hardship. You might have to acknowledge that some people you're close to are difficult and harmful and you'll need to do your best to protect yourself and your kids from them. But these troubles can be balanced by the kindness, love, and connection I know you and your family can create, maintain, and sustain, through your inherent love, appreciation, and good sense.

I've already mentioned that my childhood was unhappy and chaotic, so it won't surprise you to learn that when I was an adult, I was ambivalent about being part of a family. You might be too. But as I learned to open my heart, using the meditations and practices I've shared here, I discovered that I yearned to become part of a family—and I did. I helped create a happy one, and so can you. You, and all the members of your family, can start by making a commitment to develop personal insight, practice patience and kindness, and to reliably support and show up for each other, again and again. By doing so you'll plant seeds that will flourish and bloom throughout your life—as long as you're mindful to water them regularly with wisdom and care.

Practice Eighteen: May All Families Be Happy

You can do the following practice by yourself, but I really hope that you do it with your family members, too. It's really fun to include your children and you can adapt it as you need so everyone can participate. This exercise gladdens the mind and reconnects you to your deepest loving connection and reminds you that you're not alone. All families want to be happy and want to have the conditions for contentment, peace, and prosperity, and with this practice you can contribute to help make that happen.

1. Sit down somewhere quiet where you won't be disturbed. Most important, keep your devices out of reach, shut off your television and music, and commit to not reading, checking email, or talking for the next fifteen minutes.

2. Close your eyes. Put your hand on your heart and rest your attention on your breathing. Feel the inhale and exhale from your navel to your nose.

3. If you're sitting with your family, notice their presence. You might hear their breath or sense them sitting nearby. You can even open your eyes and smile at each other.

4. Next, put your hand on your heart. Silently, imagine you and your family in a moment of happiness and ease. Maybe on vacation, relaxing in the backyard, or watching your favorite program together. Visualize all of you connected, relaxed, and loving. Silently say, as if you're giving a gift to your family, *May we be happy*. Continue to repeat these phrases for at least five minutes.

5. Now, imagine another family, one that you know: your siblings and their kids or good friends that you've known a long time, or families that you know from church, temple, or school. Imagine this family

is standing here in front of you and silently say to them, *May you be happy*. Continue repeating and giving these blessings to this familiar family.

6. Now slowly envision all the other families in the world. Think of those who are close to you and those who are strangers to you. Imagine families everywhere, in Europe, Asia, Africa, rich, poor, middle class, small and large, old and young, married and unmarried, straight, LGBTQ, those with children and those without. Share your love across the globe, and say silently, *May all families be happy. May we all be happy*. Keep connecting to everyone and repeating these phrases for several minutes.

7. When you conclude this meditation, be sure to thank yourself. If you're practicing with your family, open your eyes, put your hands together at your heart, and offer each other a bow of appreciation.

SECTION III
HAPPY FRIENDSHIPS

CHAPTER 19

A Lucky Life

Shared joy is double joy; Shared sorrow is half a sorrow.
—SWEDISH PROVERB[1]

IT'S NOT AN EXAGGERATION FOR ME TO SAY THAT FRIENDSHIP IS MY single greatest good fortune. As an only adopted child, growing up in a chaotic and stressful environment, and lacking stable and reliable people who could appropriately care for me, I felt lonely and neglected—until I met Carol. Carol and her family moved into the house next door when I was four years old, and she and her little brother Donald became my first friends. They often invited me to their house to play, sleep over, or have dinner. A year later, when I got to kindergarten, I met more children and made more friends. With their help, I began to discover much of the love, kindness, and understanding that I missed in my own family.

I've been told many times, and perhaps you've heard this too, that your family should take priority over your friendships and, indeed, any other relationships in your life. Platitudes like "family is everything" or "family first" might sound good but hold little meaning—because not all relatives and blood relationships are reliable, kind, and caring. In fact, in many cases your friends are far more honest, loving, and dependable than many, or any, of the members of your family. This is why so many friends *become* family. And even if you're someone who is lucky enough to have tight-knit and supportive parents, siblings, kids, and spouses, you likely know they can't be everything to you: you need friendships every bit as much as you need family.

That's because friendship holds a valuable and unique role in our lives. It's a bond that's free of the history, conditioning, and dynamics that operate in families, where you might feel stuck in a role which no longer suits you or in a system that limits or strains your ability to be yourself. Friends offer you a different, more objective perspective of who you are, without the pressure, judgments, or expectations your parents and siblings have of you. Without decades of entrenched undercurrents, you and your friends are free to create a refuge, where all of you can feel close and loved, exactly as you are.

About six months after I met my now-husband, Mike, my two closest and oldest friends, Denise and Lori, came to visit me from Chicago, where they lived and I grew up. Mike was playing basketball when Denise and Lori arrived at my Brooklyn apartment around noon, and the three of us went straight to our favorite local bakery, Bien Cuit, and sat with our coffee and croissants in the sunny back garden. That's where he found us an hour later, laughing and relaxed, pleasantly chatting, and obviously enjoying our time together. When they left for the airport a few days later, Mike told me he hadn't seen me that happy and at ease before—and he was right, he hadn't.

That's because my friends have been my deepest source of healing, where I've experienced the greatest kindness, least criticism, and the most acceptance. When I'm with them, I'm more open and available to reveal myself to them than to my parents, colleagues, or strangers because I know I can do so without fear of being misunderstood or shamed—and that's what Mike observed when he was with us. The Buddha noticed this power of friendship, too. He understood that it could be a profound source of mutual inspiration and encouragement, where we can cultivate each other's virtues, wisdom, and goodness. That's why he and his students lived and studied together in close community, because, he said, good companions (also called "dear ones") ground you in reality, guide you to develop care and kindness, and help you flourish as your best self in your best endeavors. The Buddhist path regards friendship as a precious resource and emphasizes the wisdom of cultivating and appreciating it to help you create a loving and meaningful life. In the chapters in this section, I'll show you the traditional lessons I've learned from my teachers about friendship so you can enrich and enhance this treasure too.

> The next time you communicate with a good friend—via text, on the phone, having coffee together after dropping the kids at school—let them know how much they mean to you. Say to them that you appreciate their companionship, you're happy they're in your life, or just say thank you for being a friend.

Of course, friendships aren't immune to misunderstandings, disagreements, separations, or divisions. Sometimes your fears, expectations, and neediness will spoil your goodwill for others, and changes in your interests, lifestyles, and values can drive a wedge between even the closest of dear ones. But I know that you can meet these struggles with patience and learn to address them wisely, with compassion for yourself and your people, using the spiritual tools and exercises in this book. You, and all of us, can learn to meet your impatience and frustration, notice your judgments, and explore your misconceptions to repair and strengthen a struggling friendship. And you'll also learn when to use your wisdom and discernment to recognize that it's time to step back or make a change in your involvement, without ill will or anger at your friend or yourself.

Even friendships that are already steady and loving can deepen if you foster your wisest intentions with mindfulness and lovingkindness. You'll benefit from improving your connection and strengthening your bonds with patience, generosity, and gratitude. You'll see that you can maintain your connections, not out of obligation or habit, but because you recognize the value of these unique relationships. Whether you have many friends or just a few—and even if your best friend is an animal—I know you can experience the wealth of support and strength these relationships can bring to your life. My friendships have grown and flourished using the compassionate and simple trainings shared here, and yours can too.

When you rely on your dear ones, your happiness becomes sweeter and your losses lighter as you journey through life together.

There's a lovely old teaching called the Mitta Sutta [Discourse on Friends], in which the Buddha explains that excellent friendships require seven characteristics. We can use it as a guide when we meet new people or feel unsure about old friends. And we can always consult the list to ensure that we embody the qualities that a good friendship requires.

Admirable friends

1. Give what is hard to give.

2. Do what is hard to do.

3. Endure what is hard to endure.

4. Reveal their secrets to you.

5. Keep your secrets.

6. Don't abandon you in times of trouble.

7. Don't look down on you in times of loss.

You might notice that the list doesn't say that our companions need to share the same values, come from the same background, or even have common interests. What's more important for a true friendship, the Buddha says, is that we treat each other with generosity, vulnerability, diligence, and trust. You likely already know these are the skills that are necessary to make authentic and loving connections—with ourselves and others too.

Practice Nineteen: Sharing Your Blessings

In traditional Buddhist philosophy it's believed that we can create good in our life through our own actions. This good is called *merit*, and whenever we think, say, or do something that's beneficial to ourselves, others, and the world, we create it. *Merit* is sometimes translated as virtue, potential, or luck—positive energy that contributes to our well-being and helps us thrive and flourish. In some Buddhist countries, like Thailand and Sri Lanka, merit-making is highly esteemed, and individuals celebrate their good fortune—a promotion, a birthday, or a graduation—by making donations or giving gifts, both of which are exercises in generosity and kindness that generate a lot of merit.

Merit is meant to be shared—not hoarded—so whenever you produce merit, you're encouraged to give it away. In this lovingkindness meditation, you'll learn to notice and share your merit with your friends as a means to help them create positive conditions to thrive and flourish.

1. Find a quiet place where you can relax outdoors or near a window. You can lie on a blanket in your backyard, relax in a chair in your bedroom near a window, or even sit in your car.

2. Deeply inhale through your nose, bringing air all the way to your belly and exhale slowly and fully. Do this at least three times.

3. Rest your attention on the sounds entering your ears from outside. If you're sitting in your house or apartment or car, notice only what you can hear from outside of your space.

4. Put your hand on your heart. Imagine you're looking in the mirror at yourself. Smile at your reflection. Say to yourself, *May my joy increase. May I have good luck and happiness.* Repeat these phrases to yourself silently for five minutes.

5. Now remember a time recently when you were patient, gave someone a gift, or offered assistance. Remind yourself that this action created merit. Imagine that a friend is with you and silently say to them, *May my merit increase your joy, and give you good luck and happiness.* Repeat this silently for them for a few minutes.

6. Imagine you're looking at the earth from space. See this vulnerable blue planet, its atmosphere, and all its living beings. Offer your merit to everyone by saying, *May my merit increase everyone's joy, and give everyone good luck and happiness.*

7. Before you stop practicing and resume your activities, just rest for a few seconds without moving. Be sure to thank yourself for your diligence and energy.

CHAPTER 20

Embracing Differences

Respecting differences while gaining insight into our essential con-nectedness, we can free ourselves from the impulse to rigidly categorize the world in terms of narrow boundaries and labels.

—SHARON SALZBERG[1]

LUIS AND PEDRO MET IN SIXTH GRADE AT LOYOLA ACADEMY, A PRIVATE Catholic boys' school in their suburban hometown. Both came from big Mexican American families though neither were religious—and this brought them together, as they'd both felt alone in their agnosticism and rejection of most of the tenets and rules of the faith that each believed to be sexist, homophobic, rigid, and judgmental. In high school they fell into the grunge music scene, smoking pot, growing their hair, and going to Pearl Jam concerts, to the dismay of their parents, teachers, and even some of their classmates. But their lives began to diverge soon after college, when Luis bought a house in a town near where they grew up in New Hampshire, and Pedro moved to Boston. They saw less of each other, and a few years later, Pedro was surprised that Luis planned to get married in their local parish church. Confused and somewhat disappointed, he didn't understand why his friend wanted a religious ceremony, but Luis said it was simply because that's what his new wife and their families expected them to do. Despite his reservations, Pedro agreed to be the best man and enjoyed the celebration. For the next few years, the friends met at holidays and at the occasional sporting event, and though they kept their conversation away from politics, it seemed to Pedro that Luis got more and more conservative—and to Luis, Pedro was too liberal. These feelings were confirmed when Luis came to Boston for a sales conference and they met for dinner; Luis mentioned to Pedro that he no longer thought that birth control should be easily available and wanted abstinence to be taught in his kids' public schools. Pedro was shocked—and angry. He couldn't believe how much his friend had changed and told Luis he felt like he no longer knew him and accused him of being as narrow-minded and conservative as their parents. Luis was hurt that his friend was so judgmental and critical and accused him of not wanting to grow up. The meal ended without resolution and both men were hurt and upset and wondered if they'd become too different to continue their friendship.

It's certain that everything will change, and that includes people. But what do we do when we no longer feel we have anything in common with our oldest companions, or we stop sharing the same values? I know I've asked myself these questions before, and you might be wondering about it, too. Do friends need to agree on everything? Must we have the same interests and political affiliation? What if we believe our friends' views are harmful to others or destructive to the world? These questions are complicated, and especially important to consider right now, not only for our current friendships and relationships, but for how we treat everyone in our community. That's because, as I'm sure you've noticed, our society in general has become increasingly fragmented and many of us are less tolerant of those who think and live differently than we do.

Buddhism provides us with a useful pathway to help us bridge these kinds of divisions. Its teachings suggest that instead of focusing on the opinions or viewpoints we disagree about—which only leads to further separation—we emphasize and remember our *shared humanity* to bring us together. Shared humanity is what all of us have in common, despite social, cultural, geographic, and economic differences. Perhaps the most important—and obvious—thing we share is that we all want to be happy and not suffer. Everyone in the world wishes to be content, healthy, and to abide in a peaceful place with enough food and resources to live comfortably. Another thing we all share is that each of us will get older, get sick, and die, and everyone will experience loss, sadness, and grief. Remembering these profound commonalities unite you in deep compassion for the joys and sorrows you share with everyone, even people who hold differing opinions or those you don't like.

That's how Pedro and Luis were able to reconnect. They hadn't been in touch for several years, but when Pedro heard that his old friend's wife, Amanda, was diagnosed with breast cancer, his heart went out—to both of them. He knew that Luis would be worried, afraid, and in pain—because that's how Pedro would feel if his wife were sick. He called Luis and they quietly agreed to disagree on politics and religion and focus on what really mattered to them—the support, love, and compassion they shared for each other.

Despite understanding your shared humanity, it may not be possible for you to stay friends with someone whose opinions and views are too opposed to your own. You might discover that you can't justify behaviors that are unethical or harmful, and you shouldn't. All of the teachings of the Buddhist tradition, including the Eightfold Path and the Four Immeasurables are designed for you to cultivate and discern what is wholesome and to avoid what is unwholesome. Discernment is a type of wisdom that understands that certain actions will always result in harm, so we should not do them or support others who do them. For example, you can see for yourself that behavior resulting from hatred or greed will always injure—racism and war, for example, will never result in justice or peace. So when someone you know holds convictions that are dangerous or malicious, you can compassionately choose to end your relationship with them while continuing to acknowledge your shared humanity too.

If a friend doesn't share your views, it's time for listening not arguing. Don't try to change their mind or tell them they're wrong. Encourage them to share their feelings about the issues and learn to empathize with their opinions, even if you have divergent viewpoints.

I learned this directly a few years ago when Jimmy—whom I knew in high school—began telling me on Facebook that the United States had no responsibility to other nations and that we should stop sending humanitarian aid for victims of natural disasters and armed conflicts and stop assisting refugees to immigrate. At first, I attempted to explain to him why giving to other countries is an expression of generosity and morality. But then I realized it wasn't possible for me to persuade him or change his mind. Through my discernment, I know for certain that it's wise to care for others because instability can cause violence and war which affects the United States and other nations, and the destruction of the environment impacts every living creature in our ecosystem. So I ended our exchange, without anger or demands, and when I see his profile in my feed, I silently wish him peace and ease.

In many stories, the Buddha cautions his students to avoid arguments about what opinions are "right" and which are "wrong." He tells us to avoid being "disputatious" because this only results in division, ill will, and discord. That's because when we're too attached to anything—people, wishes, or beliefs—we cause ourselves pain and frustration. The Buddhist practice of nonattachment encourages us to let go of these deeply held views—to use our mindfulness and notice when we're clinging or insisting on our opinions, and to relax a little. Instead of arguing or getting angry because you disagree with someone, you can simply trust in your own good sense and have confidence in your position without trying to dissuade others from their interpretation or make them see things your way. You can kindly disagree with a friend, and even know that their outlook is foolish or harmful, without disputing their opinion, telling them they're wrong, or arguing. This is especially helpful when you feel absolutely certain that your friends are factually or morally incorrect. Instead of trying to change their minds or prove them wrong, you can use your kindness and good sense to accept that it's not up to you to make them see what they can't see or aren't ready to accept right now.

Practice Twenty: Open to Difference

If you're feeling disappointed, discouraged, or sad that someone you know is very different from you, holds views that you think are harmful, or insists they're right when you know they're not, I hope you'll try this exercise. It's to remind you of all that you have in common and all that you've shared, to help you reconnect and bring kindness, receptivity, and openness to yourself and to your relationship.

1. Start by putting away your devices and sitting down in a quiet place.

2. Feel your breath from the tip of your nose to your navel. Just let your attention rest on the gentle movement of your respiration for a moment.

3. Remember your intention for doing this practice. It might be that you don't want to feel anger about a friend, or that you want to open your heart to them, or that you want to be more patient, or let go of ill will. Whatever your motivation for doing this exercise, take a moment to understand it, say it out loud, and appreciate it. You can even write your intention down on a piece of paper to help you connect with it.

4. Think of a time when your friend offered you a kindness. This might be long ago or recently. It could be small: a text of encouragement for a new job—or large: when they fixed your car or acted as maid of honor at your wedding. Take a minute to visualize them and their action, recalling what happened and how it made you feel.

5. Now imagine your friend is sitting right next to you. Visualize their face and say to them silently, *May I be open to the way things are with you.* Repeat this for several minutes.

6. Now imagine both of you together in a happy moment, and say silently, *May we be at ease with the way things are with us.* Say this silently over and over for a few minutes.

7. Finally, just take a few conscious breaths before you conclude this meditation. Remember you can practice it anytime you feel frustrated or annoyed with someone you care about.

CHAPTER TWENTY-ONE

Sharing Loss and Sorrow

I learned that unconditional love—for ourselves and all beings— arises once we allow for the natural flow of change, and then we can welcome the continual arising of new ideas, new thoughts, new invitations. If we do not block whatever comes our way, there is no boundary to our love and compassion.

—YONGEY MINGYUR RINPOCHE[1]

WHEN CATHERINE WAS TWENTY-THREE YEARS OLD, JUST AFTER SHE finished college, she was diagnosed with terminal leukemia. Her mom had died in a car accident a decade before, and she was estranged from her dad and half-siblings, so a group of her friends came together to take care of her. Like Catherine, all were recent graduates, in their twenties, and they coordinated her care, took her to medical appointments, visited her in the hospital, and were with her when she died. Then they adopted her cats, arranged for her cremation, and organized her memorial. Though I never met Catherine, I feel like I did, because when I met her friends nearly twenty years after she died, I heard so much about her. I was touched by their closeness and tenderness with each other, which was forged through this mutual painful bond that happened when they were young. Now middle-aged professionals, when we meet for dinner they often talk about their dear friend and how hard and painful it was for her to be young and sick and how devastated they were when she died. But they also laugh so much, appreciating how they used to sneak into her hospital room and flirt with the night nurse to let them sleep over, and how happy they were that Catherine lived long enough to attend her roommate's July wedding in Wave Hill and what a perfect day they'd spent together. And they continue to be grateful to her for bringing them together.

Like Catherine, you might find that your family members aren't the greatest or easiest source of support for you, given the complicated histories and difficult dynamics you might share with them. That's why when I was listening to Catherine's friends, it reminded me of all the times I'd supported—and counted on—my friends during times of loss, grief, and unexpected change, too: when Denise was so upset after she separated from her husband and Lori and I convinced her to join us on a beach vacation where we all got sunburned and ate ice cream for lunch every day, and years later, after my father died and Steph and Craig sent me a gigantic bouquet of flowers with a care package of chocolate and sparkle pens.

It wasn't always so easy for me to deal with difficult situations—especially those involving loss and grief—because I found it overwhelming and scary. Maybe you do, too. You might notice that you hesitate to reach out to a friend who's lost a parent or gotten divorced because you're afraid of their grief; maybe you feel inadequate to respond to it appropriately because you never learned how to do it. I didn't either; my father's advice to me about these kinds of upsetting circumstances was "don't get involved," and whenever one of his friends or neighbors was in the hospital or got separated from their spouse, he avoided them. Sometimes he sent flowers or gave them money, but he didn't want to talk to them because their feelings made him uncomfortable and upset. And that's how I managed sad and challenging incidents too—until my mother got sick.

My mom was in and out of hospitals for nearly a year before she died, and through that experience I learned not only to tolerate, but to compassionately navigate loss. I'd been training as a Buddhist for several years when her health crisis began, and I used its tools to support me through it. I learned to sit down and put my hand on my heart when I felt overwhelmed, instead of reacting angrily to the medical staff or yelling at my boyfriend. It was hard at first because I wanted my distress to just disappear. But as I continued to meet my pain with patience and attention, I soon felt a growing tenderness toward myself, and slowly, I discovered how comforting it was to simply experience my gentle and nonjudgmental presence. When you learn to do this too—and I assure you, you can—your tolerance for sadness grows, and your compassion does too.

After my mom's death, I was surprised how much more easily I could empathize, listen, and understand the pain and loss of others. When my ex-boyfriend called to tell me his mom, Phyllis, had been diagnosed with Parkinson's disease, instead of giving him advice on how to find the best treatment for her, or telling him not to worry too much, I simply said, "That's very painful. How are you feeling?" I was able to hear and respond to his experience in a way that supported him and me, simply with my spacious awareness. The beautiful truth is that I discovered—just like Catherine's friends did—that sharing heartache and anguish not only alleviates your pain, but it also strengthens and deepens your connections and friendships, instead of destroying them.

If you've experienced a significant loss—the death of someone close to you, getting fired or laid off from your job, the end of a long relationship—don't be afraid to ask for help. Reach out to your friends and tell them you're struggling, find a support group, or contact www.grief.net for resources.

If you're the one going through heartbreak or grief, you might not only feel sad and overwhelmed, you might also experience shame or embarrassment. Maybe you don't want your friends to know what you're going through, and maybe you were taught, like I was, that it's humiliating and weak to ask for comfort or consolation because you should be stronger or more independent. I want you to know that nothing could be less true! All of us are dependent—we need and rely on others for everything: food, water, air, information, care. It's factually impossible to be completely separate from the world, and if you believe this delusion (it's pervasive in our culture) you're suffering because of it.

In Buddhism, bravery and strength result from compassion, not invulnerability or self-suffiency. Compassion includes a heroic willingness to open your heart when anyone you encounter is needy, distressed, weak, or in pain. Sometimes that person is you, and that's when you can use your courage and wisdom to ask for assistance and to accept it with appreciation and good sense when you receive it, even with reluctance. That's how Dave felt about accepting support from his friend Gino.

When Gino came to town to see his parents for Mother's Day, he wanted to visit Dave too, but Dave wasn't sure. He was in the middle of a divorce and had recently moved into an apartment nearby. Dave didn't want his friend to worry about him and told him that he was doing okay and he didn't have to come over but Gino insisted. When he got to Dave's apartment, the garbage was overflowing and dirty dishes were strewn on the table and the countertops. In the living room there were empty pizza boxes on the couch, and dirty socks and magazines on the floor which looked like it hadn't been vacuumed since he'd moved in. Gino moved a sweatshirt off a folding chair and sat down and said with concern, "Why didn't you tell me?" Dave replied, "I didn't want you to think I couldn't take care of myself"—at which point both men laughed loudly, and when Gino hugged him, Dave felt so relieved he began to cry.

Generosity, patience, good sense, love, joy, and all the other positive qualities, traits, and attributes of the Buddhist path are skills that everyone can learn—but all require effort. You might think this means *work*—and approach the path by demanding or insisting that you be kinder or forcing yourself to be more mindful. Obviously, this approach will just result in discouragement and exhaustion. That's why the Eightfold Path encourages you to use *viriya* or Wise Effort instead. Wise Effort is also translated as wise energy, diligence, or discipline, and if you try to harness it without consideration and compassion for yourself, then even cultivating love or joy will feel like an obligation or requirement, instead of what it really is—a choice and a blessing. When you truly practice with Wise Effort, the process of creating your positive attributes is also positive—using gladness and enthusiasm as well as persistence and dedication results in delight for your accomplishments and satisfaction in your purpose.

Practice Twenty-One: Green Tara

When someone I loved struggled with cancer, the news of her condition got worse and worse, and each day I was more stunned and overcome with shock and sadness. Finally, after learning her illness was progressing even faster than expected, I decided I would just sit down and be quiet by myself for a few hours. At first, I couldn't stop ruminating and thinking and worrying. But I kept remembering to come back to what was happening right now—the cool air from the window, my upset stomach, and all the pain and tightness in my chest. I said to myself, "Kim, you're really upset and it's okay," and felt my body relax, and I sighed. Then I said, "Tara, I surrender. I don't know what the future holds but I will trust that you'll help me meet it with wisdom and compassion. *Oṃ Tāre Tuttāre Ture Soha.*"

Green Tara is a Buddhist manifestation of compassion. Though many consider her a god or deity, it's more accurate to say she is a representation of our human capacity for compassion and love. When I pray or make wishes to Green Tara, I'm not actually asking for an outside entity to grant me something or intercede on my behalf. Rather, I'm talking to—and trusting—in my own good heart and clarity, which is sometimes hard to see. I'm also articulating to myself that not everything is in my control, and that's okay. As I make these wishes to Tara, I can sense a quieter and calmer presence inside of me, which is inside of you too.

The Green Tara contemplation is available to everyone, Buddhist or not. And I encourage you to practice it, even if it seems too religious. Sometimes submitting to something greater than yourself—even metaphorically—can ease heartache and loss and the painful insistence that we can control the uncontrollable or predict the unpredictable. The following instructions are condensed from teacher Venerable Thubten Chodron.[2]

Green Tara Practice:

1. First, put your hand on your heart and on your belly, close your eyes, and just breathe.

2. Next, visualize Green Tara is floating in front of you, in one of two forms:

    a. You can imagine her in her Buddhist form: sitting cross-legged on a lotus flower, with glowing green skin and hair and lovely warm brown eyes. She's wearing necklaces of gold and jewels, a rich silk gown, and her right leg is a bit in front of her, as if she's ready to spring into action.

    b. You can imagine Tara as a familiar saint, teacher, or loving friend. Visualize this woman sitting in front of you, looking you in the eyes with kindness, and perhaps touching your face tenderly.

3. As you look into Tara's eyes, repeat this mantra: *Om̐ Tāre Tuttāre Ture Soha.* As you do so, visualize rays of light flowing from her heart to your heart. Continue reciting the mantra for a few minutes or more.

4. Then ask Tara for support. You can tell her your wishes and ask her to help you, or surrender your worries to her.

5. Now imagine that this visualization of Tara slowly condenses and dissolves into a drop of light. This light droplet enters your forehead and into your brain, where it slowly falls down your spinal column. Imagine it moving past your forehead, throat, chest, abdomen, and finally coming to rest at your root.

6. Sit quietly for a few minutes, allowing the essence of Tara to become integrated with your essence.

7. Finally, conclude the practice by saying, *May all beings including me be free from suffering and the causes of suffering. May it be so.*

CHAPTER TWENTY-TWO

Animal Friendships

It might actually be easier for us to feel closer to animals or nature, precisely because we have made human relationships so complicated. For many people, a relationship to a pet can serve as an important source of closeness and love.
—HH THE 17TH KARMAPA, OGYEN TRINLEY DORJE[1]

I SOMETIMES SAY THAT MY BEST FRIEND IS CARMEN, A TWELVE-YEAR-old Siamese rescue cat adopted from a Brooklyn shelter. I work from home and we spend all day together, as she follows me from the bedroom to the kitchen when I wake up, springs to the countertop as I make coffee, joins me at my desk where she sits on my lap as I work. She's an affectionate and compassionate companion, and we're in tune with each other's moods and needs. If I'm feeling insecure, she senses it and snuggles up next to me, and at night when she's worried that our more dominant cat will push her off the bed, I gently gather Carmen and tuck her into the covers next to me.

I know that our relationships with animals can be as valuable and significant as those we have with other humans, and if you have pets, you understand this too. The love and support they share with us is sincere, and even their simple presence imparts comfort, joy, and pleasure—as much as any person could offer you. Indeed, no matter what type of pet you have—a dog, horse, guinea pig, chicken, cat, or any other kind of animal—you know how valuable they are to you. I even witnessed the connection between my seven-year-old niece and her goldfish, Leonard. Though of course she didn't bond with him as closely as she did with her dog and cat, Leonard was a dear member of her family. He lived in her room and when she approached his bowl, he swam excitedly in circles— something that he did for no other human. And when he died a few years later, she grieved and missed his quiet company and graceful movement.

If your only friend is a pet that's fine—unless you feel lonely, isolated, or have the need to talk. Pets aren't substitutes for people. Look for a way to socialize with other humans. Find a support group or consider joining a community that shares your interest, perhaps by joining a nearby dog-walking meetup or volunteering at your local animal shelter.

When we give and receive love with our animal friends, it can help us heal deep emotional wounds and allow us to experience the power of unconditional friendliness and support. Kyle, the owner of a coffee shop near my old apartment, deeply understands this. He'd been divorced from an emotionally abusive ex-spouse for about a year when he met Cooper, an adult collie/pit bull mix. Kyle told me he didn't think he was ready to take care of anyone but himself at the time, but Cooper needed a home, so Kyle decided to foster him. He quickly noticed that in contrast to his difficult romantic relationship, being with Cooper was simple and easy and honest. Kyle felt less lonely and was surprised to discover how deeply satisfying it felt to know that Cooper was content and happy as a result of his love and care so he adopted him. A few years later, Cooper was diagnosed with kidney disease and required Kyle to provide him with a special diet, oral medications, and weekly injections. One of the baristas at the café wondered if Kyle didn't feel resentful that his pet was so needy. Kyle laughed in surprise because he knew that his care for Cooper was as healing to him as it was to his dog.

In the Buddhist tradition, animals aren't excluded from our care or compassion or love. Indeed, there are countless stories about human-animal friendships, because Buddhism recognizes that other living creatures deserve the same respect, consideration, and compassion that we offer human beings, and with good reason—our lives are inter-dependent with theirs. When we exclude other creatures from our care and protection, we do so at a cost to ourselves. Large-scale cattle farming for meat production is one of the biggest generators of greenhouse gas emissions and contributes to global warming and climate change, and overfishing cod in the last century resulted in a drastic decline of the fish and a collapse of the local fishing industry.

Another reason we share our love with animals is because they are vulnerable to aging, sickness, and death and experience physical and emotional pain, just like we do. Many share our ability—and our desire—to give and receive affection and kindness. That's why all the types of love in the Four Immeasurables (lovingkindness, compassion, appreciative joy, and equanimity) are *indiscriminate*. This means that our circle of care not only includes all humans (our friends, enemies, strangers), it includes all life. We share our love with everyone: humans, birds, mammals, reptiles, rodents, lizards—all creatures from the tiniest to the most majestic. This might seem strange to you if you were taught, like me, that only certain animals are worthy of your respect and benevolence. You might not feel inclined to wish for the well-being of creatures that disgust you or that you fear because you learned to *discriminate* your lovingkindness—to only care about special animals like pets, dolphins, elephants, or other beautiful creatures, but certainly not rats, crocodiles, or animals raised for human consumption, like cattle or pigs. It took me a while, but now my lovingkindness includes my family, friends, Carmen the cat, pigeons, whales, cockroaches, and centipedes—and with a little practice, yours can too.

Traditional Buddhism believes in reincarnation—the theory that, after death, everyone is reborn into another body, and after that body dies, into another body, and so on. This cycle continues endlessly in a perpetual system of birth, death, and rebirth. Just because you're human now doesn't mean your next reincarnation will be human, or that your last incarnation was human either. You could be and have been many different living creatures. In fact, according to this worldview, we've all been born so often in so many different forms for such a long time that we've interacted with nearly every being that we meet in our current life—there are no strangers. That means that in past lives, your cat or dog was once your mother or father and your greatest human enemy today was once your beloved horse. I'm not sure if reincarnation is true or not, and it doesn't matter if you believe in it either, but the way you relate to other creatures will transform if you regard every being that you meet, including nonhumans, as a dear one who has meaning, value, and connection to you.

Practice Twenty-Two: For the Benefit of All Beings

Lovingkindness meditation is a progressive practice. You begin with those dearest and closest to you, like old friends and pets. Then you include frustrating family members, strangers, and finally even your *enemies*—people you don't like or who have caused you injury or harm. But the practice doesn't end there. The fullest expression of lovingkindness is when you include every being in your circle of generosity, care, and kindness, including yourself.

There are many creative ways to ensure that your practice excludes nobody. One is to imagine all the countries and areas on Earth until you've covered the entire globe with lovingkindness; another is to name different species—mammals, water beings, flying beings, humans—until all types are encompassed. The simplest is just to include one particular group, for example, widows or dogs, and then all those who are excluded from the group, in this example those who are not widows or dogs. The following is my favorite way to practice lovingkindness: by grouping creatures through the number of legs they have. It begins with the many-legged beings and concludes with those who have none. I hope you'll let yourself have fun with it!

1. Put away your devices.

2. Lie down or sit somewhere quiet where you won't be disturbed. If you're at home, tell your family not to bother you for twenty minutes.

3. You don't have to do anything right now. Just allow yourself to breathe, feel the air on your skin, notice your toes and feet. Do your best to relax just for a few minutes.

4. Beginning at the top of your head, gently sweep your attention down through your body. If your attention is swept away by thoughts or plans, gently let go of them and return to your sensations.

5. After a few minutes, put your hand on your heart and silently say to yourself, *May I be happy and safe*. Repeat this for a few minutes.

6. Now think of all the many-legged creatures—those that have more than four legs. This includes spiders, octopuses, centipedes and lots of other insects, and lobsters and shrimps, too. Try to remember all the beings you know with lots of legs. Say to them silently, *May all creatures with many legs be happy and safe*. Repeat for a few minutes.

7. Next consider creatures that have four legs. This includes most mammals and reptiles—dogs, cats, rats, crocodiles, and newts. Imagine animals you know that have four legs. Say to them silently, *May all creatures with four legs be happy and safe*. Repeat for a few minutes.

8. The next group are creatures that have two legs. This includes humans everywhere, all ages, cultures, skin colors, languages, and ethnicities. It also includes most birds—chickens, sparrows, and vultures. And chimpanzees and gorillas too. Imagine all these beings and say silently, *May all creatures with two legs be happy and safe*. Repeat for a few minutes.

9. The final group are living beings that have no legs. This means worms, snakes, and slugs, but it also means most aquatic creatures like whales, jellyfish, trout, and dolphins. Imagine all the legless beings you can remember, and say silently, *May all creatures without legs be happy and safe*. Repeat for a few minutes.

10. In conclusion, you can imagine giving your lovingkindness to everyone on Earth, including yourself. You might visualize seeing the planet from space. Say silently, *May all beings everywhere be happy and safe*. Before you stand up and resume your activities, be sure to say thank you to yourself.

CHAPTER TWENTY-THREE

The Difficult Friend

Friendship is always a sweet responsibility, never an opportunity.
—KHALIL GIBRAN[1]

BRITTANY AND LISA HAD KNOWN AMY FOR NEARLY THREE DECADES. They'd worked together at a grammar school: Brittany and Amy as teachers, and Lisa as an assistant principal. They became friends when they all joined a committee formed to offer free lunch options in the cafeteria. Brittany and Amy soon became roommates, and a few years later, Lisa and Amy were attendants at Brittany's wedding on Martha's Vineyard. Though all had long since changed jobs, they still met often, took weekend trips together when they could, and texted each other every few days. But as much as she cared for Amy, Brittany was finding it increasingly difficult to remain in touch with her. That's because Amy complained—a lot—about a lot.

On the patio at their favorite restaurant, Amy couldn't wait to tell them how awful her latest Bumble date was, or the most recent annoying comment made by the dean at her new school. Amy lamented that she'd never get to move to Arizona (something she'd been talking about for nearly a decade) because she insisted it would be impossible to sell her condo or afford a home in Phoenix, even though Lisa's sister was a Realtor and had many times offered to help her. When Brittany suggested that she consider going to therapy or apply for a new job, Amy forcefully insisted that nothing could be done about her troubles and complained that Brittany and Lisa couldn't understand what she was dealing with because they weren't single and living on their own like she was.

I bet you know what I'm talking about because you probably have an Amy in your life. A help-resistant complainer, a friend who has nothing positive to say, an unreliable colleague who cancels or doesn't show up for plans, or someone you know who is always fighting or in conflict with another person. I've had friends like this too, and like Brittany, I feel frustrated and impatient with them because they continue to make the same mistakes, perseverate about their problems instead of solving them, or seem to lack insight or interest into their own motivations or habits. I feel sure I know what they should do. But the truth is that even if you believe that your friend will feel better when they change jobs, listen to their spouse's advice, or start physical therapy for their bad back, it's not in your power to make them do it. You can't know for certain what is best for another person and trying to do this will just increase the resentment and annoyance you feel. And, after all, not everyone wants your advice.

> You are not obligated to continue a friendship that that is abusive, cruel, or manipulative. Use your wisdom and good sense to understand when you're being harmed and take steps to protect yourself from it.

Jay realized this recently when his colleague LJ mentioned—again— that the project he was working on was beyond his skill set, and he didn't think he'd finish it on time. Jay told him again that he'd be happy to review it for him, but when LJ shook his head, Jay wanted to scream. He didn't understand why his colleague wouldn't let him help him—until Jay's wife pointed out that LJ hadn't *asked* for help. Only then did Jay realize that all he was being asked to do was to listen, and if LJ wanted assistance, he would ask. But Jay still felt angry about it and just couldn't understand why his friend wouldn't listen to him.

Earlier in the book, I mentioned the Buddhist quality of equanimity and how practicing it helped me to stop feeling responsible for my mother. Translated from the ancient Pali word *upekkha*, equanimity means understanding your limitations and knowing that what other people do is not up to you. Being equanimous with a difficult friend doesn't mean you have no concern for them—you do—but you don't have to insist that they do what you say or resist accepting who they are. Instead, you can remember that you have no control over their decisions, beliefs, and choices, and that's okay. You can still wish them well and keep your heart open and your mind steady with patience and love instead of aggression or frustration. And you can offer them your wisdom and blessings like I do when I'm with a difficult friend. As soon as I notice that I'm feeling tight and irritated, I stop talking, take a breath, and silently say, *May you find a true source of happiness* or *May you find peace exactly where you are.*

It also helps me to remember that my friend isn't trying to be annoying or behave badly. In fact, the people we find difficult are usually suffering; they're fearful, lonely, anxious, or depressed. They don't know how to comfort themselves or relieve their feelings, and your criticism, annoyance, or exasperation is probably going to make them feel worse, and you, too. It's smarter and kinder to remember that they're stressed and upset and approach them with love and easiness. This doesn't mean it's your responsibility to take care of them, or allow them to treat you badly, but rather to set aside your frustrations and expectations of them and meet them as they are without trying to fix or change them. Then you can decide what is the wisest action you can take for both of you. Sometimes the best thing to do is just to listen and empathize. Other times it might be to separate yourself and limit your contact for a while, to regain your patience and peace of mind. And though it's hard to watch another person struggle unnecessarily, when you understand the limits of what you can do *and* what your friend can do, you'll create a new dynamic that is less frustrating, more open, and gentler to both of you.

Wise Speech not only includes speaking truthfully, listening patiently, and refraining from saying hurtful words, it also includes not gossiping. That's because gossip—talking about a person in a way you would never say to them directly—is, by definition, divisive, unkind, or untrue. Gossip might seem like a harmless way to discharge irritation about someone you know, but it reinforces negative or cruel opinions and fuels feelings of annoyance or ill will toward the person you're talking about.

I've done plenty of gossiping in my life and never really considered its effects. But when I started my Buddhist training, I decided to stop doing it. At first it was such a spontaneous habit that I didn't even notice I was nattering until after I'd started speaking. But now I use a simple mindfulness technique whenever I feel the urge to talk about another person behind their back. I gather all my awareness on my closed lips and feel the sensations where my upper lip and lower lip meet. As long as I'm paying attention to my lips touching, I can be sure I'm not talking—or gossiping.

Practice Twenty-Three: Be Open

There have been many moments when I've felt frustrated or annoyed with a friend, and I've learned that when I feel that way, I've lost my connection—to myself. When you're bothered or irritated by a friend, this meditation will help you get back in touch with your good heart, rediscover your wisdom and compassion, and bring kindness to yourself and this difficult person, too.

1. Find a quiet place and sit down. Leave your devices off and out of your reach.

2. Close your eyes and feel yourself breathing. Listen to the sounds outside of where you're sitting. Stay still and let these external sounds come to you.

3. Keeping your eyes closed, listen to the sounds inside or near where you're sitting. If it's quiet, you might just hear silence or your own breath or heartbeat. Keep your attention on these nearby sounds.

4. Next, put your hand on your heart and imagine you're looking at yourself in a mirror. See your face and look in your own eyes and feel your presence with your hand on your chest. Say to yourself silently, *May I be open to my struggles and appreciate my joys.* Repeat these phrases silently to yourself for a few minutes.

5. Now imagine your difficult friend. Visualize they're sitting near you, not as the adult they are now, but as a child. Make a connection to this innocent young girl or boy, and say to her or him silently, *May I be open to your struggles, and appreciate your joys.* Say these phrases silently as though you're giving a gift to this child, your friend.

6. You can continue practicing for as long and as often as you like. Before you conclude, be sure to show yourself appreciation with a deep sigh, a pat on your own back, or putting your hands together in front of your heart and bowing.

CHAPTER TWENTY-FOUR

Transforming Envy and Jealousy

Your work is to find out what your work should be and not to neglect it for another's. Clearly discover your talent and attend to it with all your heart.

—THE BUDDHA[1]

WHEN I WAS TWENTY-THREE YEARS OLD, I MOVED TO NEW YORK CITY, where I met Sofia. At the time, I was waitressing while deciding whether to go to graduate school or intern at a publishing house, and Sofia was just finishing her degree in art history at Barnard. I lived in a fifth-floor rent-stabilized walkup apartment in an old tenement in the Lower East Side, and my boyfriend had just moved out, so Sofia became my roommate. For the next few years, while I struggled to figure out what to do with my life—taking then leaving waitressing gigs for temp jobs, struggling with depression and finally going into psychotherapy, quitting smoking, and taking morning yoga classes, Sofia was becoming more and more successful. She began working at a small auction house but quickly got a position at a famous sculpture gallery in Chelsea, started dating a prominent magazine editor, and finally moved out of my place and into a spacious and sunny loft in Soho that her parents helped her buy. I tried so hard not to be envious because I really liked Sofia—she was a genuine and caring friend and was funny, kind, and smart. But I was always comparing my life to hers, and it just didn't measure up. I felt ashamed of my jealousy and became unable to offer her joy or even congratulate her on her successes. I was convinced she had so much and I so little that I couldn't listen or empathize with her worries or plans. We began to see less and less of each other and eventually our friendship ended.

For a long time, I thought I was a bad person for feeling this way, but what I didn't understand then was that envy is a signal of deep suffering. Whenever it arises, it creates resentment and insecurity, and though my feelings weren't "wrong," they were causing me pain. As long as I continued to measure my life against Sofia's or anyone else's, I would always believe I was lacking something. And because I thought that what she had was "better" than what I had—more worthwhile, prestigious, and pleasant—it was impossible for me to recognize and value all the good things that I already possessed. I discounted my talents, my material comfort, my other relationships, and all the love in my life because I just couldn't see them.

I bet you've done this too—since everyone I know is comparing themselves to and competing with other people, sometimes even our dearest friends. That's because so many of us feel inadequate and unworthy and believe that if we only had more of something—money, time, aptitude, influence, beauty—it would make us feel content, happy, and loved. This is one of the reasons why learning Buddhism has been so transformative for me—its teachings insist that we pay attention to what is true. And the truth is that the accomplishments of others don't diminish me—or you—or lessen your chances of realizing your own aspirations. In fact, in what feels like an impossible paradox, I can assure you that you will have more happiness in your life when you celebrate your friends, rather than begrudging their achievements. This quality, called *mudita*, which means "appreciative joy," is one of the types of love included in the Four Immeasurables.

Mudita is when you feel delight and happiness for the good things that happen to other people. Though you might not know it, you've certainly experienced *mudita* before, most obviously at weddings or graduations, where you've likely felt glad, hopeful, proud, and excited for the couple or the graduate. Like lovingkindness, compassion, and equanimity, *mudita* is boundless and indiscriminate, and you can deepen it with practice so that you can experience the joy of everyone's success—even those you envy. When you're able to share in the joys of others, instead of comparing what they have to what you have, you'll feel less left out or abandoned when those close to you attain or receive something you wish you had too. Then you don't have to believe something is wrong with you or that someone else is better than you, because you'll understand that their success has nothing to do with yours. If your friend wins the lottery or has a seemingly perfect and wonderful family, their luck doesn't hinder or stop you from having your own good fortune. In fact, the more you experience *mudita*, the more likely you'll view your friends' blessings as evidence that the possibility of good luck and happiness exists, and if it happened to them, it can happen to you, too.

Like all the practices in this tradition and in this book, *mudita* requires that you pay attention—to your relationship to yourself and others, too. As you do, you'll notice that those you envy not only have joys, but like all human beings, they also have sorrows. You'll see that even those who seem to have everything have problems and worries, despite their wealth, popularity, or endowments. If I had been a bit more mindful when I was younger, I would have easily seen that Sofia was a very anxious and insecure person who rarely felt at ease, no matter how talented she was or how many good things happened to her. If I'd noticed this, she likely would have seemed more relatable to me, and I might have had more compassion for her, and instead of distancing myself from her friendship, I could have reached out and brought her closer to me.

When you feel seized with envy or jealousy, stop and feel it. It's a powerful emotion, often including a hot and burning energy in your body, and your immediate reaction might be to push it away or ignore it. I encourage you to take a quiet, slow breath instead. Then, put your hand on your heart and say, "I see you envy and I'm not going to leave you." Repeat as often as needed.

Feelings of jealousy and envy can increase if people say things to you like "you should live your best life," "follow your dreams," or "live up to your potential," but you feel you aren't or believe you can't. Just remember that we all have different circumstances. You have particular family, societal, genetic, and environmental influences that have contributed to who you are—your physical health, personality, talents, and your emotional makeup are distinctly yours. So are your privileges, opportunities, and skills. Instead of emulating other people and trying to be like them or get what they have, you can use your wisdom to recognize your own particular abilities, blessings, and even limitations. This is how you create a real "best life," which has little to do with material goods or achievement. A real best life is one in which you develop your limitless capacity for love, wisdom, compassion, and joy so you can truly connect—with yourself, friends and family, strangers, your enemies, and even animals.

The late Zen teacher Roshi Bernie Glassman describes the inimitable and original qualities you have as *ingredients* and suggests that instead of wishing you were like someone else, you celebrate who you are. He encourages you to "take the ingredients you have and make the best meal you can."[2] If you pay attention to your talents, resources, and intentions, use them skillfully and avoid comparing yourself to others, you'll create *not the life you think you should have*, but the authentically beautiful life that is waiting for you to see it and share it with the world.

Practice Twenty-Four: Honoring Your Feelings

Recently, two separate students mentioned to me how challenged they felt by their own emotions. One struggles with envy, and the other is mourning the loss of his mom, and both just want the feelings to go away. They're not alone. Nearly everyone I know—including me—gets impatient, annoyed, or frustrated by emotions, thinking "Why do I keep getting angry?" or "When am I going to stop feeling so jealous?"

To deny, bypass, or fight with anything inside of ourselves will simply increase our suffering and make unwanted experiences even more powerful, insistent, and overwhelming. That's because before your difficult emotions can resolve, they need to be heard and cared for—by you. So if you're having trouble listening to your own feelings, sensations, or thoughts, I hope you'll try this brief lovingkindness practice to reconnect and open your heart to yourself.

1. Shut off your devices and leave them out of reach. Commit to not using your phone for the duration of this meditation.

2. Lie down in the most comfortable place in your home: your bed, the old couch in the basement, the cool wooden floor in the living room.

3. Don't do anything. Just lay quietly.

4. Put your hand on your heart, take a few breaths, and think of someone who loves you. Imagine they are sitting near you.

5. Silently say to this loving person, *May you care for yourself with ease. May you be open to the way things are. May you be at peace.*

6. After a few minutes, feel your beautiful presence, and imagine looking right into your eyes and silently say, *May I care for myself with ease. May I be open to the way things are. May I be at peace.*

7. Finally, give your love to all of us struggling beings everywhere, saying, *May everyone—may we care for ourselves with ease. May we be open to the way things are. May we be at peace.*

Chapter Twenty-Five

Planting the Seeds for Happy Friendships

People who are more socially connected to family, to friends, to community, are happier, physically healthier, and live longer than people who are less well connected. It's not just the number of friends you have, and it's not whether or not you're in a committed relationship, it's the quality of your close relationships that matters. Living in the midst of conflict is really bad for your health. Living in the midst of good, warm friendships is protective.

—Dr. Robert Waldinger[1]

I've mentioned the importance of sangha or community and *kalyanamitras* or spiritual friendships several times in this book, but when I first began studying Buddhism, I didn't think other people were important to it at all. At the time, I was attending dharma talks (public classes that include meditation and discussion of Buddhist principles and philosophy) several nights a week in New York City at several different centers. I was very glad to attend, happy to read the recommended texts, and eager to listen to the teachers. But I had no interest in getting to know any other participants or to make friends. I always sat in the back by myself, and although many students stayed to mingle and chat after the program, I left as soon as it ended. Though my mind was steadier than it had ever been, and I felt much kinder to myself and patient with my friends and family, I couldn't understand why all the books and teachers insisted that community and friendship were so essential to the tradition. It certainly didn't feel necessary to be with other people in order to get good at mindfulness and lovingkindness, as I was easily practicing and learning by myself.

But one day, about six months after I started, I went to a talk with a popular Buddhist teacher at a downtown mindfulness center. It was held in a big loft and felt crowded with over fifty people sitting on the floor on cushions or on folding chairs, forming a semicircle around a small platform where the instructor, an older Buddhist nun, sat. She talked about the Buddhist concepts of impermanence and change and guided a traditional breath-focused meditation. When it ended, she asked if we had any questions, and a man in his mid-thirties raised his hand. When he began to speak, he faltered, and in a voice thick with emotion, asked "But what about the pain when things change?" and tears ran down his cheeks until he added, "I'm getting divorced," then he sobbed. A powerful quiet blanketed the room as he cried, but the silence wasn't from embarrassment, judgment, or rejection. Everyone—including me—simply listened and opened our hearts to his grief. Nobody offered advice or platitudes like "you'll get over it" or "divorce takes time," or made a joke to try to lighten the mood. And a few minutes later, when the teacher finally spoke, she kindly affirmed his struggles and said, "Yes, the heartbreak of change is very painful. But it doesn't mean there is anything wrong." In that moment, I understood why community and friendship are valuable—they're powerful tools to assuage pain and heal suffering.

Since then, I've experienced the healing power of collective compassion many, many times—at Buddhist centers, with friends, and even on the subway with my fellow New Yorkers. And though I'm still an introvert by nature—most comfortable by myself—I now know I'm influenced and affected by everyone I encounter, and they're influenced and affected by me. I realize how powerful my kindness, patience, and presence can be, and I think you understand this too. I hope that the practices in this book help you realize your beautiful qualities of wisdom, patience, and love and will inspire you to not only connect with your dearest people, but to also consider expanding your definition of friendship and community. I encourage you to create a sangha wherever you are—with your friends, family, or strangers—at church, at school, or at work. Plant seeds of compassion with your words and deeds, water them with mindfulness and lovingkindness, and watch them grow. With your interest and care they'll contribute to a global sangha in the future, where all people meet as friends, without indifference, bias, or cruelty, where we recognize and support everyone's humanity, with empathy, consideration, and benevolence. *May it be so!*

Practice Twenty-Five: May All Friendships Be Happy

If you want to feel joy and happiness, I recommend that you do this meditation, and I hope the next time you're with someone you care about, you invite them to practice it with you. It connects you to all the people who are your dear ones, reminds you of the delight created by this special bond, and enables you to share in the affection and love everyone experiences thanks to our loving friendships.

1. Sit down somewhere quiet where you won't be disturbed. Keep your devices out of reach and commit to not reading, checking email, or talking for the next fifteen minutes.

2. Close your eyes. Put your hand on your heart and rest your attention on the movement of your chest as you breathe. Notice the sensations of the inhale and exhale from your navel to your nose.

3. If you're sitting with a friend, notice their presence. You might hear their breath or sense them nearby. Then adapt the rest of this exercise to include your friend instead of imagining someone. If you're not practicing with a friend, simply skip to the next step.

4. Keep your hand on your heart and silently imagine a friend is here with you. Perhaps they're sitting next to you or you visualize that you're together in a pleasant place—at the beach, in a park, in your family's living room. Imagine you're holding hands, and repeat silently, *May we be happy.* Continue to say this phrase for at least five minutes, while you imagine seeing your friend and holding their hand.

5. Now think of a group of friends—your siblings and their dear ones, or your children and other kids playing together. Visualize that they're standing in front of you and feel their presence. Silently say

to them, *May you be happy*. Continue repeating these blessings, as if you're giving them a gift.

6. Next, begin to include all friends. First, envision this group with you and your friend, all together in a lovely place, perhaps outdoors or at a party. Now invite all of your friends and visualize they're here, too. Start to imagine all the friends everywhere throughout the world, rich, poor, middle class, old and young, all different languages and cultures, those newly acquainted and those who grew up together. Picture all these dear ones from around the globe are here with you too. Perhaps you feel them or imagine you're all in big sunny peaceful field outdoors. Share these phrases, saying silently: *May all friendships be happy. May we be happy.* Keep imagining a world of happy connected people, repeating these phrases for several minutes.

7. As you conclude this meditation, be sure to thank yourself. If you're practicing with your friend, open your eyes, put your hands together at your heart, and offer each other a bow of appreciation and love.

Afterword

Where Will You Leave it?

I always bear in mind that my mission is to leave behind me the kind of impression that will make it easier for those who follow.

—Marian Anderson[1]

Soon after takeoff on a flight from Chicago to New York on a cold wintry day, the aircraft I was on encountered considerable turbulence. The captain announced, "Flight attendants to the jump seats," and my heart sank. I almost stopped breathing as the plane jolted; my stomach churned and my hands began to shake. I'd been nervous since I boarded the plane because I don't like to fly, but now I was terrified. I reached for my headphones and put them on my ears and pressed play. Soon I heard the soothing voice of the late Vietnamese Zen teacher Thich Nhat Hanh. While I listened, I gathered my attention to his words and followed his instructions to be mindful and attentive to myself and to stay present with my body and my senses. With my hand on my chest, I felt my heartbeat and breathed more deeply, becoming a bit more relaxed. Then I said to myself, "Kim, this flight is not in your control," and sighed.

Thich Nhat Hanh reminded me that everything is impermanent—including my life. I thought about what would happen if the plane crashed, how panicked I would feel, and how terrible it would be for the people who love me. I worried about Mike, Lori, my niece, and my students and wondered what would happen to them. Then, in my mind, I suddenly heard the voice of my mother-in-law, Cathy, asking me,

"Where would you leave it?" Cathy often used this expression to explain how people influence each other, especially parents and children. It was sort of the Irish equivalent of "the apple doesn't fall far from the tree." When her niece Cae became a high school soccer star, Cathy laughed and said of Cae's mother, "Sure, where would she leave it?" because she'd been a champion athlete in her youth. And when a neighbor's son was arrested for burglary, she said of his father, "Of course, where would he leave it?" because he'd been an abusive and cruel man to his family. As the plane continued its bumpy ascent, I wondered, "Where would *I* leave it?" I thought about what I've given to other people and realized that I'd done a pretty good job of leaving my best qualities—my love, wisdom, goodness—with my most important relationships. I felt a little easier knowing that whatever I have of value will be left with those I love: Mike, Lori, Madeleine, Carmen, Renee, Mona, Steph, many dear ones, my students, and my community. I felt a little easier with this realization, and even after the plane landed safely at LaGuardia, it has stayed with me.

I hope this book will help you consider where—and what—you'll leave with your partner, family, friends, and all you encounter in your precious life. To whom will you leave your good sense, humor, affection, wisdom, and empathy? With whom will you share your love, diligence, and generosity? As you pay closer attention to the people and animals in your life, you'll know without a doubt they are your most valuable treasures. And you'll notice that the way you think, speak, and treat them has a profound effect on them and on you. Though there will be many times when you forget this truth, and say something unkind or get impatient with your spouse or child, if you say to yourself "Where do I want to leave it?," you'll be able to reconnect with your finest intention, and start over, again and again.

When I embarked on my journey, decades ago, to understand why I struggled to connect with other people, I was a troubled young woman wondering why I felt alone, sad, and not good enough. I thought I would need to fix myself before I could have satisfying relationships, and you might feel this way too. But as I developed insight and understanding through therapy, community support, Buddhism and mindfulness and lovingkindness practices, I discovered I could also heal through my relationships. You can, too. That's what all the practices in the book are for—developing your capacity to give and receive the transformative power of love.

Remember, restoring and repairing your connections isn't a linear process—you'll continue to feel sad, angry, unsure of yourself or self-critical sometimes, but don't get discouraged. If you're mindful of all your many blessings and bring compassion to your struggles and suffering, you'll always be tethered to your good sense and loving heart. You'll be able to trust yourself: trust that you're motivated by a wish to be genuinely happy, and trust that it's possible to create the conditions for a beautiful life for yourself and everyone in it, even during the most difficult and painful circumstances. Then you'll be sure of *where you left it*, just as I am. You'll leave it with the people who mean the most to you. They'll inherit your most valuable possessions—your goodness, patience, generosity, and wisdom—and your legacy will help protect them through the joys and sorrows of life with grace and ease.

Appendix A

Mindfulness Meditation Instructions

MINDFULNESS MEDITATION IS A SIMPLE TECHNIQUE OF BEING PRESENT with whatever is happening inside and outside of you in each moment. By bringing your attention to what's occurring right now, you'll be less distracted by worries about the future or regrets about the past. You'll be able to focus on whatever is in your mind, body, and heart, whether you like it, dislike it, or find it dull. You'll develop your capacity to react less out of habit and more from choice and good sense. Anyone can practice mindfulness; it doesn't require special equipment, it's not religious, and you can do it anywhere. I suggest you practice these instructions for fifteen minutes each day.

Step 1: Get Still
> Sit, stand, or lie down somewhere that is relatively quiet where you won't be interrupted, keeping your hands still. Sit as comfortably as possible, with an upright spine and breathing easily, in a chair or a cushion on the floor. Your eyes can be open or closed.

Step 2: Say Hello
> Take a minute or two to ask yourself, "How *am* I right now?" A response may come in the form of words, images, and/or bodily sensations—just notice what comes up, but try not to get too caught up in it. Allowing whatever is arising to arise can help us approach our body and mind with compassion.

Step 3: Come to Your Senses

Bring your attention to your body. Notice your feet touching the ground, your seat, the palms of your hands. Experience your shoulder blades, the back of your head. Allow sound to enter your ears.

Step 4: Find an Anchor

Choose an object of attention on which to focus. This is most commonly the breath, but you can use sounds or the feeling of your feet touching the floor. If using the breath, find one place in your body where you can feel your inhalations and exhalations: the tip of your nose, your abdomen, your chest. Experience the sensations and movement of your body breathing and allow it to anchor you in the present moment.

Step 4A: When Thoughts and Emotions Arise

It's very common to notice that attention only stays with the breath or body for a few cycles before it wanders away. If you notice your mind remembering or planning something see if you can simply come back to *this one breath that you are breathing right at this moment.* Don't worry if you have to do this a hundred times in a single meditation session; each time you bring yourself gently back to your breath, you are strengthening your concentration, the ability to direct your mind back to the present moment.

Step 5: Say Thank You

At the end of the meditation session, take a moment to appreciate and acknowledge the benefits of the practice you just did—not only for yourself, but for everyone you have contact with today.

Appendix B

Lovingkindness Meditation Instructions

LOVINGKINDNESS MEDITATION IS A BUDDHIST PRACTICE DESIGNED TO help you cultivate concentration, wisdom, and compassion. It's translated from Pali (the language of the early Buddhist texts) from the word *metta*, which means friendship, goodwill, and lovingkindness. The intention of offering lovingkindness is to develop your wise heart by connecting with other beings and recognizing their wish to be happy, their desire not to suffer, and their deep struggles. Lovingkindness meditation is traditionally offered to five beings in a progressive order from easiest to love to hardest to love. The conventional order is self, beloved benefactor, dear friend, familiar stranger, and someone you dislike. Note that you may experience love, happiness, sadness, annoyance, crabbiness, boredom, or any other feelings during this meditation. This is normal and you don't need to chase or create "positive" emotions. When you notice you've lost the connection with the person or the phrases, just gently return your attention to the practice and begin again.

Traditional Lovingkindness Phrases:

> May I/you/we be safe.
>
> May I/you/we be happy.
>
> May I/you/we be healthy.
>
> May I/you/we live with ease.

Step 1: Find a comfortable place to sit on a chair, or lie down on the floor or a couch. Close your eyes and bring your attention to the physical sensations of your body. Notice sounds entering your ears; feel the feeling of your feet; connect with the sensation of your breath as it rises and falls on your belly, and experience the light that's entering your eyelids. Pay attention to coolness, tension or tightness, warmth, pulsing, or even pain. You don't have to change anything or fix anything, just patiently be mindful of whatever is arising.

Step 2: Put your hand on your heart. Anchor your attention here and make a connection with yourself. You can imagine seeing yourself as an adult or a child; or just have a sense of your own presence here with you. Now say the following phrases silently, as though you're giving yourself a gift: *May I be safe, may I be happy, may I be healthy, may I live with ease.* Continue to repeat these phrases. If you get distracted and stray from the words, simply notice this, come back to a sense of yourself, and start the phrases again.

Step 3: Let go of this connection to yourself. Repeat steps 1–3 for each of the other five beings: beloved benefactor, dear friend, familiar stranger, and someone you dislike. After you've offered lovingkindness for each of these people, you can conclude the meditation. You might be tempted to skip the person you dislike, or only do the practice briefly for the stranger, but try to spend the same amount of time practicing with each being. At the end of the meditation, be sure to take a moment to offer lovingkindness to everyone: *May all beings be safe, may all beings be happy, may all beings be healthy, may all beings live with ease.*

Appendix C

Meeting Difficult Emotions Exercise

YOU CAN PRACTICE THIS WHENEVER YOU'RE SUFFERING FROM DISTRESS-ing feelings. Be sure to find a quiet spot where you can sit or lie down comfortably, put away your devices, and stop talking. Just let yourself rest for a bit. The idea is not to get rid of, transform, or fix your feelings, but rather to welcome and befriend them, with compassion and patience.

1. Feel what you're feeling. As you inhale, experience any physical sensations as well as thoughts/judgments/beliefs that let you know what emotion is arising. As you exhale, let yourself relax into them. Do your best to not resist anything that's arising.

2. Name what you're feeling. "Anger is arising," "I feel fearful," "Sad-ness," "This is depression," "Rage is arising," "I feel so mad," "I feel lost," "I am in pain." Refrain from saying, "I am" as in "I am enraged," "I am sad," because you are not your emotion. Emotions are transient, impermanent experiences that change and cease, but your wise presence is abiding and steady.

3. Validate what you're feeling. Say to yourself, "Anger is here and it's okay," "This grief is welcome here," "This is a moment of suffering," "I feel very upset and vulnerable and it's okay to feel this," "I'm open to this experience." Use your own words to comfort and soothe yourself. Let yourself open your heart to whatever you're feeling, without rejecting or trying to understand or resist.

You can use this practice sequentially, moving from step 1 to 2 to 3, or just use whatever step seems most useful in the moment, moving from the different steps as needed. Note that you are not trying to get anywhere or achieve anything! You are learning to let yourself be, to be with your life as it is in this very moment.

Please note: If you feel too overwhelmed to continue while you're practicing, open your eyes and pay attention to your senses. Name five things that you see and five things you can hear. You might decide to take care of yourself by having a cup of tea in silence or taking a walk without your devices.

APPENDIX D

The Four Immeasurables

THE FOUR IMMEASURABLES ARE FOUR QUALITIES OF LOVE THAT EXIST in all human beings. Known in Buddhism as the Brahmaviharas, they have a literal meaning as the "highest dwellings"—states of mind which create the happiest life. The Four Immeasurables can be developed and perfected, and unlike emotions, which come and go, they are abiding qualities.

Lovingkindness	Pali word: *Metta*
	Meaning: Goodwill, love
	Quality: Wishing for yourself and others to be happy
	Cause: Seeing that all beings want to be happy, noticing the goodness in people
	Opposite: Hatred
	Less obvious opposite: Attachment, desire, clinging
	Phrase: May you be happy
Compassion	Pali word: *Karuna*
	Quality: Feeling suffering and wishing to alleviate it
	Cause: Seeing the helplessness of others in suffering
	Opposite: Cruelty
	Less obvious opposite: Pity, burnout
	Phrase: May you be free from suffering

Appreciative Joy

Pali word: *Mudita*

Quality: Joy at the good fortune of others

Cause: Seeing successes of others

Opposite: Jealousy

Less obvious opposite: Comparison

Phrase: May your joy never cease

Equanimity

Pali word: *Upekkha*

Quality: Even-mindedness

Cause: Seeing that actions have outcomes

Opposite: Indifference

Less obvious opposite: Greed and anxiety

Phrase: All beings are the owners of their karma (the outcome of their actions); their happiness and unhappiness depend on their actions, not on my wishes for them

APPENDIX E

Dedication of Merit Practice

The Great Dedication of the Bodhisattva
Through the merit collected through all that I have done,
May the pain of every living creature
Be completely cleared away
May I be the doctor and the medicine
And may I be the nurse
For all sick beings in the world
Until everyone is healed.

—SHANTIDEVA[1]

MERIT—ALSO CALLED LUCK, VIRTUE, OR POTENTIAL—RESULTS FROM our beneficial thoughts, speech, and behaviors. Dedicating the Merit is a mindfulness exercise used to appreciate these skillful actions and remember that doing them is valuable, since the merit they generate has a positive impact on you and everyone you meet. Traditionally, merit is *dedicated* (given, shared, or transferred) to all beings, to help create positive causes and conditions for everyone to thrive and awaken.

HOW TO DEDICATE THE MERIT
You can share merit anytime something that you think, say, or do is generous, wise, or kind—after meditation practice, when you give your seat to an elderly person on the bus, and when you're grateful for a meal.

Below are examples of dedications you can recite, and be sure to create your own, too.

- *I give any goodness arising from my actions to the well-being of all living beings.*
- *Through my merit, may all beings be joyful and at ease.*
- *May the virtue of my actions benefit all beings and dispel hatred, greed, and delusion from the world.*
- *I dedicate the positive energy from this act of kindness to all those who are suffering; may it help them find peace and comfort.*
- *I offer my merit to everyone living in places of war and violence. May all be safe, protected, and free from fear.*
- *Whatever merit is created through this action, may it bless everyone.*

DEDICATING THE MERIT TO A DECEASED LOVED ONE

In some Buddhist countries, merit is offered to deceased ancestors, with the intention to support them wherever they might be. You can offer your merit to anyone you love who has died by reciting this phrase:

> *I offer any merit generated by my actions today to my dear [name]. Through my efforts, may [name] be safe and peaceful, and dwell in happy realms.*

Notes

EPIGRAPHS

1. The Buddha, *Madhupindika Mangala Sutta* [The Discourse on Blessings], translated from the Pali by Ṭhānissaro Bhikkhu, https://www.dhammatalks.org/books/Chanting Guide/Section0051.html.

2. Robert Aitken, *Zen Vows for Daily Life* (Boston: Wisdom Publications, 2018), 10.

INTRODUCTION

1. Yoko Ono, *Feeling the Space*, Apple Records SW-3412, 1973. Liner notes.

CHAPTER ONE

1. Jon Kabat-Zinn, *Wherever You Go, There You Are: Mindfulness Meditation in Everyday Life* (New York: Hachette, 2003), 48.

CHAPTER TWO

1. Dang Nghiem, "Rehearsing Suffering," *Tricycle Magazine*, March 21, 2021, https://tricycle.org/article/sister-dang-nghiem-suffering/.

CHAPTER THREE

1. J. Krishnamurti, *The Book of Life: Daily Meditations with Krishnamurti* (San Francisco: HarperOne, 1995), 13.

CHAPTER FOUR

1. Thich Nhat Hanh, *Anger* (New York: Riverhead Books, 2001), 124.

CHAPTER FIVE

1. Jack Kornfield, *Buddha's Little Instruction Book* (New York: Bantam, 1994), 68.

CHAPTER SIX

1. Ajahn Chah, *The Collected Teachings of Ajahn Chah* (Northumberland: Aruna Publications, 2011), i.
2. Sylvia Boorstein, "One Simple Practice That Changes Everything," Garrison Institute, May 29, 2017, https://www.garrisoninstitute.org/one-simple-practice-changes-everything/.

CHAPTER SEVEN

1. Brian Cox and Nicole Ansari-Cox, interview by Caroline Scott, "Brian Cox and His Wife: We Had Four Years That Were Pure Hell," *The Times of London*, February 25, 2024, https://www.thetimes.co.uk/article/brian-cox-and-his-wife-we-had-four-years-that-were-pure-hell-wczcs3d59.

CHAPTER EIGHT

1. Sensei Wendy Egyoku Nakao, "A Blessing for The Journey (Buddhist Prayer)," Bearing Witness, accessed May 12, 2024, https://bearing-witness.eu/a-blessing-for-the-journey/.
2. Jane McLaughlin-Dobisz, "The Quickest Way to Clean Potatoes," Lion's Roar, June 1, 2023, https://www.lionsroar.com/the-quickest-way-to-clean-potatoes/.

CHAPTER NINE

1. Venerable Thubten Chodron, "LR13 Bodhisattva Ethical Restraints, Auxiliary bodhisattva vows: Vow 30–36," The Gradual Path to Enlightenment (Lamrim), Thubten Chodron website, accessed May 12, 2024, https://thubtenchodron.org/1993/08/far-reaching-attitude-wisdom-benefit-others/.

CHAPTER TEN

1. Rainer Maria Rilke, *Letters to a Young Poet*, trans. M. D. Herter Norton (New York: Norton, 1954), 54.

CHAPTER ELEVEN

1. Tenzin Gyatso, His Holiness the 14th Dalai Lama, "His Holiness the Dalai Lama Spends the Day on Capitol Hill," March 7, 2014, accessed May 26, 2024, https://www.dalailama.com/news/2014/his-holiness-the-dalai-lama-spends-the-day-on-capitol-hill.

CHAPTER TWELVE

1. Laura Bridgman, "Ending Relationships with Wisdom," *Tricycle: The Buddhist Review*, April 14, 2023, https://tricycle.org/article/ending-relationships/.
2. Shantideva, *A Guide to the Bodhisattva Way of Life*, trans. Vesna A. Wallace and B. Alan Wallace (Ithaca, NY: Snow Lion, 1997), 47.

CHAPTER THIRTEEN
1. Bhante Henepola Gunaratana, *Loving-Kindness in Plain English: The Practice of Metta* (Boston: Wisdom Publications, 2017), 109.

CHAPTER FOURTEEN
1. Gabor Maté, *In the Realm of Hungry Ghosts: Close Encounters with Addiction* (Berkeley, CA: North Atlantic Books, 2011), 3.

CHAPTER FIFTEEN
1. Sherwin Nuland, "The Biology of the Spirit," interview by Krista Tippett, *On Being*, March 6, 2014, https://onbeing.org/programs/sherwin-nuland-the-biology-of-the-spirit/.

CHAPTER SIXTEEN
1. Terrence Real, quoted in Maggie Jones, "A Couples' Counselor Takes On 'Normal Marital Hatred,'" *New York Times*, January 26, 2022, https://www.nytimes.com/2022/01/26/magazine/terry-real-marriage.html.

CHAPTER SEVENTEEN
1. Dipa Ma, "Dipa Ma's Dharma Talks," Dharma Seed, accessed May 26, 2024, https://dharmaseed.org/teacher/54/.

CHAPTER EIGHTEEN
1. Charlotte Joko Beck, *Everyday Zen: Love and Work* (New York: Harper & Row, 1989), 189.

CHAPTER NINETEEN
1. Josh Ingram, *Everything Is Symbolic: 366 Days, One Thought at a Time* (Bloomington, IN: Westbow Press, 2017), 5.

CHAPTER TWENTY
1. Sharon Salzberg, *Real Love: The Art of Mindful Connection* (New York: Flatiron Books, 2017), 102.

CHAPTER TWENTY-ONE
1. Yongey Mingyur Rinpoche, *In Love with the World: A Monk's Journey through the Bardos of Living and Dying* (New York: Random House, 2019), 130.
2. Thubten Chodron, "Green Tara," Venerable Thubten Chodron, June 5, 2007, https://thubtenchodron.org/2007/06/medtation-tara-front/.

CHAPTER TWENTY-TWO
1. Ogyen Trinley Dorje, *Interconnected: Embracing Life in Our Global Society* (Boston: Shambhala Publications, 2017), 87.

CHAPTER TWENTY-THREE
1. Khalil Gibran, *The Prophet* (New York: Alfred A. Knopf, 1923), 61.

CHAPTER TWENTY-FOUR
1. The Buddha, *The Dhammapada*, trans. Anne Bancroft (London: Penguin Books, 1997), verse 166.
2. Bernard Glassman and Rick Fields, *Instructions to the Cook: A Zen Master's Lessons in Living a Life That Matters* (New York: Bell Tower, 1997), 42.

CHAPTER TWENTY-FIVE
1. Robert Waldinger, "What Makes a Good Life? Lessons from the Longest Study on Happiness," TED Talks, filmed November 2015 at TEDxBeaconStreet, Brookline, MA, https://www.ted.com/talks/robert_waldinger_what_makes_a_good_life_lessons_from _the_longest_study_on_happiness.

AFTERWORD
1. Marian Anderson, *My Lord, What a Morning: An Autobiography* (Champaign: University of Illinois Press, 2002), 201.

APPENDIX E
1. Adapted from Shantideva, *A Guide to the Bodhisattva Way of Life*, trans. Vesna A. Wallace and B. Alan Wallace (Ithaca, NY: Snow Lion, 1997), 98.

About the Author

Kimberly Brown is a meditation teacher, author, and speaker whose work explores the transformative power and wisdom of love. A Buddhist student for many years, she leads classes and retreats that emphasize the power of traditional compassion and kindness techniques to reconnect us to ourselves and others and guides individuals to create meaningful relationships through self-compassion, mindfulness, and personal insight. Kimberly teaches at meditation centers online and in person and mentors and trains mindfulness teachers.

She is the author of *Steady, Calm, and Brave: 25 Buddhist Practices for Resilience and Wisdom in a Crisis* and *Navigating Grief and Loss: 25 Buddhist Practices to Keep Your Heart Open to Yourself and Others*. Kimberly writes a popular Substack newsletter and is a regular contributor to *Tricycle: The Buddhist Review* and other publications. She lives in New York City. You can learn more about her work at www.meditationwithheart.com.

9 781493 086603